| APPROXIMATE DISTANCES IN KILOMETRES | GOBABIS | GROOTFONTEIN | KARASBURG | KARIBIB | KEETMANSHOOP | LÜDERITZ | MARIENTAL | OKAHANDJA | ONDANGWA | OSHIKANGO | OTAVI | OTJIWARONGO | RUNDU | SWAKOPMUND | TSUMEB | VIOOLSDRIF | WALVIS BAY | WINDHOEK |
|---|---|---|---|---|---|---|---|---|---|---|---|---|---|---|---|---|---|---|
| GOBABIS | | 657 | 889 | 390 | 701 | 1041 | 473 | 279 | 873 | 941 | 566 | 448 | 912 | 559 | 629 | 983 | 593 | 208 |
| GROOTFONTEIN | 657 | | 1130 | 489 | 942 | 1282 | 714 | 378 | 300 | 368 | 83 | 201 | 255 | 658 | 56 | 1224 | 692 | 449 |
| KARASBURG | 889 | 1130 | | 863 | 188 | 528 | 416 | 752 | 1354 | 1422 | 1047 | 929 | 1385 | 1032 | 1110 | 137 | 1066 | 681 |
| KARIBIB | 390 | 489 | 863 | | 675 | 1015 | 447 | 111 | 625 | 693 | 318 | 200 | 744 | 169 | 381 | 957 | 203 | 182 |
| KEETMANSHOOP | 701 | 942 | 188 | 675 | | 340 | 228 | 564 | 1166 | 1234 | 859 | 741 | 1197 | 844 | 922 | 282 | 878 | 493 |
| LÜDERITZ | 1041 | 1282 | 528 | 1015 | 340 | | 568 | 904 | 1506 | 1574 | 1199 | 1081 | 1537 | 1184 | 1262 | 622 | 1218 | 833 |
| MARIENTAL | 473 | 714 | 416 | 447 | 228 | 568 | | 336 | 938 | 1006 | 631 | 513 | 969 | 616 | 694 | 510 | 650 | 265 |
| OKAHANDJA | 279 | 378 | 752 | 111 | 564 | 904 | 336 | | 602 | 670 | 295 | 177 | 633 | 280 | 358 | 846 | 314 | 71 |
| ONDANGWA | 873 | 300 | 1354 | 625 | 1166 | 1506 | 938 | 602 | | 68 | 118 | 236 | 555 | 794 | 244 | 1448 | 828 | 673 |
| OSHIKANGO | 941 | 368 | 1422 | 693 | 1234 | 1574 | 1006 | 670 | 68 | | 186 | 304 | 623 | 862 | 312 | 1516 | 896 | 741 |
| OTAVI | 566 | 83 | 1047 | 318 | 859 | 1199 | 631 | 295 | 118 | 186 | | 118 | 338 | 487 | 63 | 1141 | 521 | 366 |
| OTJIWARONGO | 448 | 201 | 929 | 200 | 741 | 1081 | 513 | 177 | 236 | 304 | 118 | | 456 | 369 | 181 | 1023 | 403 | 248 |
| RUNDU | 912 | 255 | 1385 | 744 | 1197 | 1537 | 969 | 633 | 555 | 623 | 338 | 456 | | 913 | 311 | 1479 | 947 | 704 |
| SWAKOPMUND | 559 | 658 | 1032 | 169 | 844 | 1184 | 616 | 280 | 794 | 862 | 487 | 369 | 913 | | 550 | 1126 | 34 | 351 |
| TSUMEB | 629 | 56 | 1110 | 381 | 922 | 1262 | 694 | 358 | 244 | 312 | 63 | 181 | 311 | 550 | | 1204 | 584 | 429 |
| VIOOLSDRIF | 983 | 1224 | 137 | 957 | 282 | 622 | 510 | 846 | 1448 | 1516 | 1141 | 1023 | 1479 | 1126 | 1204 | | 1160 | 775 |
| WALVIS BAY | 593 | 692 | 1066 | 203 | 878 | 1218 | 650 | 314 | 828 | 896 | 521 | 403 | 947 | 34 | 584 | 1160 | | 385 |
| WINDHOEK | 208 | 449 | 681 | 182 | 493 | 833 | 265 | 71 | 673 | 741 | 366 | 248 | 704 | 351 | 429 | 775 | 385 | |

First edition published in 2003 by Map Studio
www.mapstudio.co.za
0860 10 50 50

**HEAD OFFICE**
Cornelis Struik House
80 McKenzie Street
Cape Town
Tel: 021 462 4360

PO Box 1144
Cape Town, 8000

**SALES OFFICES**
Map Studio Johannesburg
7 Wessel Road, Rivonia
Tel: 011 807 2292

Map Studio Cape Town
Unit 7, M5 Freeway Park
Maitland
Tel: 021 510 4211

Map Studio Durban
Shop 3A, 47 Intersite Avenue
Umgeni Park
Tel: 031 263 1203

ISBN: 1 86809 611 4
10 9 8 7 6 5 4 3 2 1

Printed and bound by
Trident Press (Pty)Ltd.

Copyright © 2003 in text: Map Studio
Copyright © 2003 in maps: Map Studio
Copyright © 2003 in photographs:
Photographers as credited (below)
Copyright © 2003 Map Studio

**Photographic Credits:**
**Jéan du Plessis:** All images with the exception of:
**Martin Harvey:** p6 (top), 26, 42 (top)
**Ian Michler:** p8 (bottom)
**Struik Image Library/**
  **Nigel J. Dennis:** p46
**Struik Image Library/**
  **Peter Pickford:** p10 (bottom)
**Willie & Sandra Olivier:** p28

All rights reserved. No part of this publication may be reproduced, stored in a retrieval system or transmitted, in any form or by any means, electronic, mechanical, photocopying, recording or otherwise, without the permission of the publishers and copyright holders.

Although every effort has been made to ensure that this guide is up to date and current at time of going to print, the Publisher accepts no responsibility or liability for any loss, injury or inconvenience incurred by readers or travellers using this guide.

**Map Studio Tourist team:**
Dénielle Lategan
Elaine Fick
Elmari Kuyler
John Loubser
Lois O'Brien
Maryna Beukes
Myrna Collins
Ryan Africa
Simon Lewis

Special thanks to Claudia dos Santos, John Hall and Willie and Sandra Olivier for their contributions.

**Been there, done that?**
Please let us know if you find any interesting information on your travels through Namibia or notice any changes. We'll reward the 10 best contributions with a copy of this guide when we update it.

Send your contributions to:
Simon Lewis
Map Studio Tourist
PO Box 1144
Cape Town 8000

or e-mail tourist@mapstudio.co.za

# NAMIBIA

# Introduction

# Introduction

Namibia, land of shifting sand, is a rough diamond on the African coast waiting to be cut and polished by any eager travellers making their way through this vast land. The treacherous Skeleton Coast lures you in, while Sossusvlei's giant waves of red sand mystify you, along with the numerous ghost towns (the social scrapyards of past glories in the world of diamond mining), drawing you ever closer with the promise of stories untold. There's wildlife in abundance and some of the natural world's most breathtaking landscapes, dramatic vistas and awe-inspiring caves to explore, although the Fish River Canyon must take pride of place as one of the world's great natural wonders. Some of the most desired national parks on the continent beckon the traveller, who'll usually be welcomed with open arms by the sub-2-million population who inhabit this ancient land, among them the legendary Bushmen who still sail barefoot across Namibia's great seas of sand. People come to Namibia to lose themselves yet, lost in all this space, many instead succeed only in finding themselves.

*"If your mouth turns into a knife, it will cut off your lips."*
*"The trees never meet (but people do)." – Namibian proverbs.*

# Historical Historical Historical Hist

### A LONG, LONG TIME AGO ...
Evidence of Stone Age occupation of Namibia exists in rock paintings estimated to be 25,000 years or older. Centuries later various groups of Bushmen (San hunter-gatherers) wandered in and settled parts of this vast expanse of land, and later Khoikhoi (the ancestors of the Nama), Bantu-speaking tribes, Hereros, Basters and Owambos made their home in Namibia.

### TAKE ME TO YOUR LEADER
Namibia's long history is of human courage, African tribal migration, settlement and conflict, a position as a strategic military stronghold along the African coastline, colonial exploration and exploitation by Britain, Germany and South Africa. UN-supervised elections were held in November 1989 and Namibia became independant on 21 March 1990. Independence and a period of blissful co-existence brought every promise for a bright future, despite some minor political instability and sporadic acts of violence. Almost four times the size of Great Britain, Namibia is one of Africa's most sparsely populated countries, largely owing to the arid nature of this low-rainfall area.

### COMINGS AND GOINGS
The 1480s were a busy time along Namibia's coast as first Diego Cão (a Portuguese navigator) planted a stone cross (padrão) at Cape Cross in 1486 (roughly 130km north of Swakopmund), followed two years later by Bartolomeu Dias at present-day Lüderitz (then Angra Pequena, or Little Bay). The spot where Dias erected his cross was appropriately named Dias Point. Considering the proliferation of British, German and Portuguese influences on Southern Africa, it's ironic that a Swedish adventurer and explorer (named Charles John Andersson) should coin the name South West Africa in his travel journal, a name which stuck, albeit with the somewhat temporary adjustment to German South West Africa, when Otto von Bismarck proclaimed the country a German protectorate in 1884).

Neighbouring South Africa sent forces in to overthrow the Germans during World War I, and thus brought the territory under their administration after the War. In 1966 SWAPO (the South West African People's Organisation) took up arms against the occupying forces of their 'rulers', and after much fighting and years of strife, free and fair elections were arranged following the implementation of United Nations Resolution 435 in 1989. SWAPO won at the polls that same year, thus signalling independence for the land after more than a century of foreign rule. Long-time advocate for independence, Dr Sam Nujoma, became his country's first president, and remains in office to this day (June 2003).

*Cormorants nesting on a wrecked ship on the treacherous Skeleton Coast. Many a ship has run aground on this bitter coastline.*

*Bushman rock paintings at Twyfelfontein.*

> *"The earth is not ours, it is a treasure we hold in trust for future generations."*
> Old African proverb.

## Historical

### DIVIDE AND RULE
After independence Namibia was divided into 13 regions: the north comprised Omusati, Oshana, Ohangwena and Oshikoto; the Kunene lies in the north-west; Kavango and Caprivi in the north-east; the central part is made up of Erongo, Otjozondjupa, Omaheke, Khomas and Hardap; and, finally, there is Karas in the south.

Namibia's democratic constitution is highly regarded by the international community, and the country is ruled by a multiparty parliament, with the overriding policy of national reconciliation and unity striving to embrace the noble concepts of tolerance and respect for differing political views, as well as racial and ethnic harmony. Power is divided between the executive, the legislature and the judiciary under the constitution.

### THE ART OF DIPLOMACY
Namibia hosts the following diplomatic missions: Algeria, Angola, Botswana, Brazil, China, Congo, Cuba, Egypt, the European Union, Finland, France, Germany, Ghana, India, Indonesia, Italy, Kenya, Libya, Malawi, Malaysia, Mexico, the Netherlands, Nigeria, Portugal, the Russian Federation, South Africa, Spain, Sweden, Great Britain and Ireland, the United States of America, Venezuela, Zambia and Zimbabwe.

### LANGUAGES
English is the official language, but with numerous different tribes as well as colonial influences, it's hardly surprising to find a multitude of languages spoken throughout Namibia. Bantu languages are spoken by the Owambo, Herero, Kavango, Caprivians and Tswana; the descendants of colonial explorers and masters speak one or more of Afrikaans, German and English (although many Namibians can communicate in one or more of these three languages); and Khoisan languages are spoken by the Bushmen (or San), Nama and Damara people.

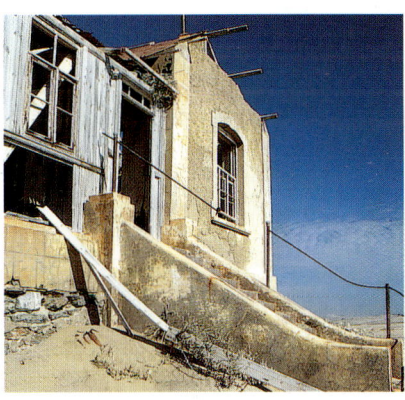

### POPULATION
Based on figures from the official 2001 census, Namibia's population swelled by over 400,000 people during the previous decade, reaching a high of more than 1,800,000 people. Interestingly, there are 50,000 more women than men. The most densely populated region is the Khomas (which includes Windhoek), with over a quarter of a million people, little more than a 100 'head' ahead of Ohangwena. The Kavango region occupies third spot, lagging 50,000 'heads' behind. Unfortunately, it's not a good country for individuals who suffer from agoraphobia (fear of open spaces), as Namibia enjoys one of the world's lowest population densities – on average there are less than two people per square kilometre.

*Namibia's ghost towns offer a window back into the country's diamond mining boom days. Bogenfels (top) and Kolmanskop (left) are both popular tourist attractions.*

*Namibians work in many different fields, ranging from the hunter-gatherers to formal farmers, in addition to a highly-skilled and diverse urban population.*

# People People People People Peop

*Himba women boast refined features, elaborate hairstyles and traditional adornments.*

*Herero women wear distinctive Victorian-style dresses and interesting headwear.*

THE CAPRIVIANS number around 80,000 and live in the Caprivi Strip. They are mostly subsistence farmers who make their living from cultivating crops, keeping cattle and fishing. These resourceful people are adaptable to the seasons: those living on the eastern floodplains of the Zambezi and Chobe rivers move seasonally, depending on the level of the floods.

Namibia's COLOURED community, along with the Basters, hails from the Cape Province in South Africa: both speak Afrikaans as their home language, although with different accents and dialects. Many are fishermen who ply the waters around Walvis Bay for their livelihood, while there are a large number of well educated coloureds, many of whom enjoy professional employment.

THE DAMARA are proud to be one of the country's oldest cultural groups, and from their ranks come many politicians who are among the most eloquent in Namibia's parliament. Their traditional homeland, Damaraland, was renamed the Erongo Region after independence in 1990, with a population numbering over 100,000.

THE HERERO migrated to Namibia centuries ago. They suffered great population losses during the colonial wars and in the 1904/5 Herero Uprising. Pastoral cattle breeders, they have retained their bonds of family life and tribal solidarity despite the wartime losses and proudly celebrate their national consciousness with a festival on Maherero Day in Okahandja every August, which includes a display of military pomp through the town's streets.

THE HIMBA are a semi-nomadic tribe of pastoralists based in the Kunene region. They live in cone-shaped 'homes' made from saplings, palm leaves, mud and dung. Proud yet friendly, these famously beautiful people are tall, slender and statuesque. They adorn themselves with bracelets, anklets, necklaces, iron belts and beautiful beads made from shells. The women protect their skin from the harsh desert sun by coating their bodies with red ochre and fat.

The Kavango River provides a lifeline for THE KAVANGO people, whose numbers have swelled to over 200,000, causing 'domestic overcrowding': on average, six and a half people live in each household! Many of the younger generation are migratory farm labourers, miners and urban workers, while those who remain closer to home ply the Kavango for fish, cultivate crops on the surrounding fertile plains or tend their cattle.

Also known as the San, Namibia's hunter-gatherer BUSHMEN are around 35,000 strong in numbers and enjoy a proud tradition as great storytellers, musicians, mimics and dancers. Their forefathers wandered South Africa's plains for thousands of years, leaving a wealth of rock art and engravings (notably the White Lady painting found in the Brandberg, as well as Twyfelfontein, the bushmen's equivalent of the Louvre) to stake their claim as one of Namibia's oldest peoples. Some of their paintings date back almost 30,000 years. A large proportion of the Bushmen now live a 'normal' life in villages, while some continue to enjoy a traditional, nomadic existence (mostly in Botswana).

*Great storytellers and poets, the Namas of the southern region find their language on the list of "Languages in Danger of Disappearing".*

## People People People People Peop

THE NAMA are Namibia's only pure Khoikhoi descendants. Certain distinctive characteristics, such as the women's small and slender hands and feet, make the Khoikhoi easily distinguishable. Nama have a natural talent for music, poetry and prose. An example of a traditional dance is the well-known Nama "stap". Numerous proverbs, riddles, tales and poems have been handed down orally from generation to generation. Nama women are highly skilled in sewing. Their embroidery and appliqué work, today regarded as a traditional art form, consists of brightly coloured motifs inspired by their rural environment and lifestyles. The content of their work is often expressive and humorous, as seen in the colourful, traditional patchwork dresses that the Nama women wear.

OWAMBO is a collective name for a number of tribes living in central northern Namibia and southern Angola. Of the nine Owambo tribes, the Kwanyama group is the largest. The most striking feature of the traditional Owambo social system is the predominance of matrilineal descent, which determines the laws of inheritance and succession, as well as post-marital residency. As a result of external factors such as the Christian doctrine, migrant labour and economic independence, there has been a distinct shift towards a patrilineally organized society.

THE REHOBOTH BASTERS can trace their roots back to the day Jan van Riebeeck's settlers first set foot at the Cape of Good Hope in South Africa. The children that resulted from the meetings of the European settlers and the Khoisan were branded "Coloureds" or "Bastards". In 1868 almost 100 Baster families migrated to Namibia, ultimately putting down roots at the hot-water springs called Rehoboth. Today the Baster community consists of approximately 72,000 people. Their mother tongue is Afrikaans and, at their own request, they have been registered as Rehoboth Basters. The Basters regard themselves as a separate community from the Coloureds by virtue of their unique history and the fact that they have been living in their own territory for more than a century.

THE TOPNAARS are a hardy people of Nama origin who have lived on the banks of the Kuiseb River for many years. Belonging to the Khoikhoi people, they speak the Nama language with its guttural clicks and high musical pitch. Central to their culinary tradition is the !nara melon, a large and nutritious fruit which is endemic to the Namib. The !nara melon is believed to enjoy certain medicinal properties.

*An elderly Nama man in Keetmanshoop enjoying his pipe, perhaps while trying to solve one of the many age-old Nama riddles.*

THE TSWANA are Namibia's smallest cultural group, numbering around a mere 8,000. Namibia's rural Tswana live in The Corridor, a narrow strip along the border with Botswana, where they are involved in cattle farming. Many of them have bought commercial farms in the Gobabis district.

THE WHITES (descended from European stock and almost all urban-dwellers and farmers) number around 100,000 of Namibia's population, and the majority are Afrikaans-speaking, with German- and English-speakers making up the rest. Roughly 150 Portuguese families (originally from Angola) still call Namibia home.

*Kids in the Caprivi area take a moment to smile for the camera, despite the pain of a broken arm.*

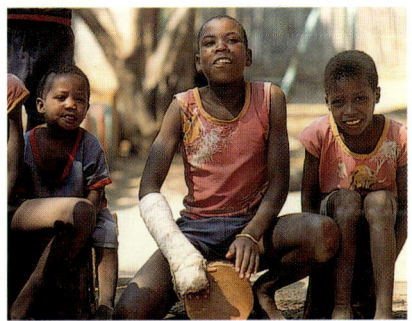

9

*"It never rains, but it pours" seems to sum up Namibia's unreliable rainfall patterns over much of the country for much of the year.*

## Nature Nature Nature Nature Natu

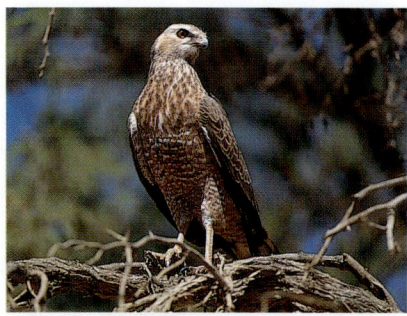

*The greater kestrel is able to hover in the air as it watches the ground beneath it for prey.*

### THE SIZE OF IT
Namibia covers an area of almost 825,000 km², in parts as wide as 1,440km and in others as narrow as 350km. You'd need more than 5,700km of measuring tape to accurately measure its perimeter; over 1,500km is coastline (from the mouth of the Cunene down to the Orange River mouth). Namibia also controls an exclusive economic zone of some 200 nautical miles off its coast, which amounts to well over half a million square kilometres of ocean.

### QUITE A RELIEF
A large portion of Namibia consists of a wide open plateau that spills into neighbouring countries at altitudes of between 900m and 1,300m. In parts massive escarpments jutt up from around the coast, the incisions were created over centuries by geological processes as well as the effects of erosion caused by vast river systems, for example in the Fish River Canyon. Aside from becoming president, the highest point a Namibian can reach is by climbing the 2,579m high Brandberg ('burnt mountain'). Namibia offers geologists endless pleasures, not least because so many of its spectacular rock formations are so beautifully exposed. Notable among these are the granite hills of the Spitzkoppe, which are remnants of great masses of magma that were forced into the earth's crust around 130 million years ago when the Gondwana supercontinent started breaking up to separate Namibia from South America.

### BEAUTIFUL BIRDS
Well over 600 species of bird have been recorded (11 endemic), with around 500 breeding in Namibia. Notable endemic species include the Herero chat, Monteiro's hornbill, Damara tern, rockrunner, long-toed plover and the greater swamp warbler. The majestic African Fish Eagle is found near water (as well as on the country's coat of arms), while the sociable weaver will enchant birdwatchers with its amazing system of communal nests – which it constructs in trees or on telephone poles – that can house hundreds of birds (some nests have survived for many decades). The brightly coloured malachite kingfisher, with its short tail and relatively long, red beak, is one of hundreds of species that grace the waters of the Caprivi region.

**Left:** Two beetles scurry along the desert sand.
**Right:** An armoured ground cricket.

*Elephants enjoying a drink at a local waterhole.*

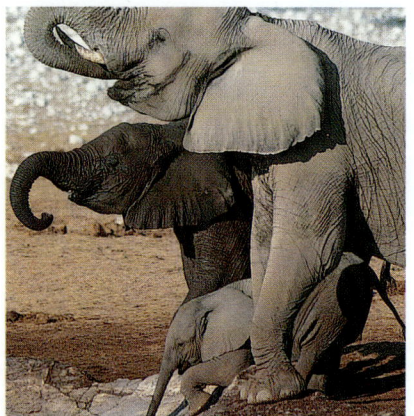

### AN ABUNDANCE OF WILDLIFE
Namibia enjoys a glorious wildlife population, with numerous species of game throughout the country, including eight endemic species of mammal (among them the black-faced impala, various mice, gerbils and bats). The big game includes leopard, lion and cheetah, in addition to elephant, rhino (white and black), hippopotamus and giraffe, as well as buffalo, Burchell's zebra and Hartmann's mountain zebra. The numerous species of antelope include eland, the greater kudu, roan and sable antelope, gemsbok, wildebeest, waterbuck, lechwe, sitatunga, red hartbeest, nyala, springbuck, impala, reedbuck, oribi, bushbuck and the

*The long-horned gemsbok can survive for long periods without water and can endure temperatures greater than 45 °C.*

# Nature Nature Nature Nature Natu

5kg Damara dik-dik, which only stands up to 40cm high on its stick-like legs. Jackals, hyaena, wild dogs and warthogs will also put in an appearance on many a wildlife expedition, as well as dassies (rock hyrax), chacma baboons and vervet monkeys. The harsh landscape naturally limits the variety and abundance of wildlife to some extent, yet equally it provides the perfect survival conditions for a number of endemic animals. The Namib desert boasts a wide range of *toktokkies* (tenebrionids) and other beetles (such as the 'fog-trapping' beetle), as well as lizards (Skoog's lizard burrows to safety in the sand with a unique corkscrew motion) and a wide range of other interesting insects and reptiles.

## HARD-HEADED FLORA

Namibia's dramatically different climates (from the coast to the harsh interior) create an environment that caters for a wide range of plant life, although the land is best known for its hardier species which have overcome the elements to thrive. Most famous is probably the endemic Welwitschia of the Namib desert, which can live from 500 to 2,000 years, one of the oldest known plants in the world. There are more than 120 tree species, including the umbrella-shaped camel thorn, the baobab, quiver trees (or kokerboom), marula, paper bark trees, mopane, figs, leadwood, jackalsbessie, Boesmangif (bushman's poison) and Makalani palms. Other plant life includes reeds and palms on the floodplains and the common driedoring flower (three-thorned flower). A fascinating array of lichens (there are more than 100 kinds throughout Namibia, some of which are endemic) can be found in the desert – these rely totally on moisture from the coastal fog for their survival. In all, Namibia has more than 200 endemic plant species, including the lithops (commonly known as the flowering stones). Other well-known plants include the *halfmens*, the elephant's foot and a number of dwarf succulents which are found near Lüderitz.

**Top:** *Flowering lithops.*
**Above:** *The welwitschia is an ancient plant of the Namib region that can live for more than a thousand years ... yet in all that time it will produce only two leaves.*

*Bushmen once used the unusual hollow branches of the quiver tree (kokerboom) as quivers to hold their arrows.*

11

*Namibia's dramatic and treacherous terrain promises modern explorers stiff challenges and unforgettable adventures.*

# Activities Activities Activities Acti

### SAND'S UP
Namibia's coastal dunes provide endless enjoyment for visitors, and are one of the best places in the world to enjoy sand skiing and sand-boarding – the idea is to push off the top of a dune and lie on the board as it slides down. Speeds easily reach 70kph. Dune-boarding may seem more refined, but it requires more skill to stand up on a small surfboard as it shoots down the side of a dune. Quadbiking involves riding 4-wheel motorcycles over and around the dunes. Though these organized trips are well regulated, the reckless use of quad bikes is increasingly damaging the fragile environment, and harming the coastal wildlife.

### SADDLE UP
Namibia has perfect conditions for horse riding, with routes crossing mountains, bush and wooded areas to desert plains and dunes. Alternatively, for a more Arabian experience, camel riding is available in places along the coast. For something completely different, and authentically Namibian, try an exciting donkey-cart drive, the traditional transport of the Topnaar people.

### TAKE THE PLUNGE
Adding an exhilarating dimension to a visit to the Namib desert is a trip in a hot-air balloon. For those individuals who enjoy taking their lives into their own hands and having adrenaline pumping through their veins, skydiving over land and sea is the answer. Paragliding enthusiasts occasionally undertake powered paragliding excursions along the coast.

*Top: 4WD trips through the desert sands might seem like a ticket to ride wild, but respect for the environment and caution for your personal safety should be uppermost in your mind.*
*Above: Desert hikes are one of the ultimate human tests against the elements.*

### OVER WATER
White-water canoeing has taken off in a big way on the Cunene River, but it's advisable to join a tour offered by an experienced adventure company if you're not experienced. Between Ruacana and Epupa there are rapids at Ondorusu and Enyandi, while Epupa Falls is set in scenic surroundings and is blessed with interesting vegetation and bird life. Canoeing safaris are offered down the Orange River, departing from Noordoewer or Aussenkehr and ending at Aussenkehr or the Fish River mouth respectively.

### UNDER WATER
Dragon's Breath Cave (on Harasib farm) lays claim to the world's largest known subterranean lake. To explore it you will need valid cave diving gear and qualifications and more courage than the average person. Harasib Cave and Lake are reached through an opening found on Ghaub Mountain, and both are worth exploring. The lake has an amazing natural display of stalactites and stalagmites. Lying 24km away from Tsumeb is the 76m

*Quadbiking on Namibia's dunes is an increasingly popular pursuit and there are outlets between Swakopmund and Walvis Bay.*

*Namibia offers a wide range of activities, from sedate family trips to high-adrenaline, blood-curdling adventures requiring great skill and courage.*

## Activities

deep Lake Otjikoto (also only for qualified divers) which will yield a treasure trove of abandoned weapons and armaments dumped here after World War I: great wreck diving for the experienced diver. On the whole, Namibia's coast presents tough conditions for scuba divers, with visibility ranging from half a metre up to usually no more than four metres. To add to the visual difficulty, temperatures in these waters range from 9°C to 17°C.

### CASTING YOUR LINE
Aspects that make coastal angling from the beach especially enjoyable are the peaceful desert environments and the uncrowded beaches. Namibia's dams in the interior offer several options for those wishing to try their hand at freshwater angling. The far eastern tip of the Caprivi, at the confluence of the Chobe and Zambezi rivers, is regarded as a tiger fishing paradise second to none.

*Sunset fishing on an uncrowded beach, with the desert sands behind you, will help clear the mental cobwebs from most city slickers' heads.*

### HUNTING
Namibia's abundant wildlife attracts hunting enthusiasts from afar to partake in trophy and safari hunting, bird hunting, as well as the ancient art of bow hunting. Written permission must be obtained from the farmer whose land your hunting party intends using before the authorities will issue a hunting permit. Note that the official term 'huntable game' strictly excludes any protected animals.

### FOUR–WHEEL DRIVE
There are countless four-wheel drive opportunities in this sandy and rocky landscape, both supervised and unsupervised. Some of the more popular and challenging include: the Dorsland Trek 4x4 Route, Isabis 4x4 Trail, Saddle Hill, Topnaar 4x4 Trail, Conception Bay Route and the Naukluft Route.

### TAKE A HIKE
Owing to high summer temperatures, tough terrain and scarcity of water, hiking in Namibia requires careful planning. Hiking is not advisable in the summer months when temperatures often exceed 40°C. Some of the best destinations and trails include: the Fish River Canyon (one of Southern Africa's top five), the Naukluft Hiking Trail, the Ugab River Hiking Trail (in the south of the Skeleton Coast Park), the Dassie Trails Network, the Sweet Thorn Hiking Trail, the Tok Tokkie Trails, the Waterberg Hiking Trail and the Waterberg Wilderness Trail.

### MOUNTAINEERING & ROCK CLIMBING
Spitzkoppe's vast granite dome rises about 700m above the desert plains between Windhoek and Swakopmund. Also referred to as Namibia's Matterhorn, the Spitzkoppe – with its almost perpendicular slopes – is one of the great mountaineering opportunities in Africa. Brandberg is a sought-after area for both mountaineers and backpackers. Due to the extremely rugged terrain and limited water, excursions should only be undertaken by experienced and fit backpackers. Abseiling is also gaining popularity due to some of Namibia's spectacular rock formations.

*Hot air balloon rides offer visitors spectacular views of the Namibian landscape.*

13

## Towns Towns Towns Towns To

Most travel guides promise that Namibia's towns (especially the "small little holes in the ground" out in the middle of nowhere) are good merely for stopping, stretching and stocking up on petrol and some niceties. Of course, it all depends how you look at it and what you're looking for! You won't find the CRASH-BOOM-BANG sights and sounds that draw the horrible hordes to the junk-food destinations. Thank your lucky stars: that's not what makes Namibia unique. The towns speak of a heritage shared across cultures and oceans, and there's no rush here: nothing is going to dash off before you get to it. If you tune into Namibia's frequency her beauty will go bang...crash...boom in tiny ripples through your soul. Drift. Wander around small museums in tiny towns. Take 10 minutes to look at the quaint memorials to bygone heroes. Ask the locals about the weather, and the best place to make a braai. This is not an 'instant' holiday spot, it's an adventure waiting to be lived.

*Namibia's capital is a modern, vibrant African city whose high-rises and pedestrian shopping malls speak of prosperity and progress.*

# Windhoek Windhoek Windhoek

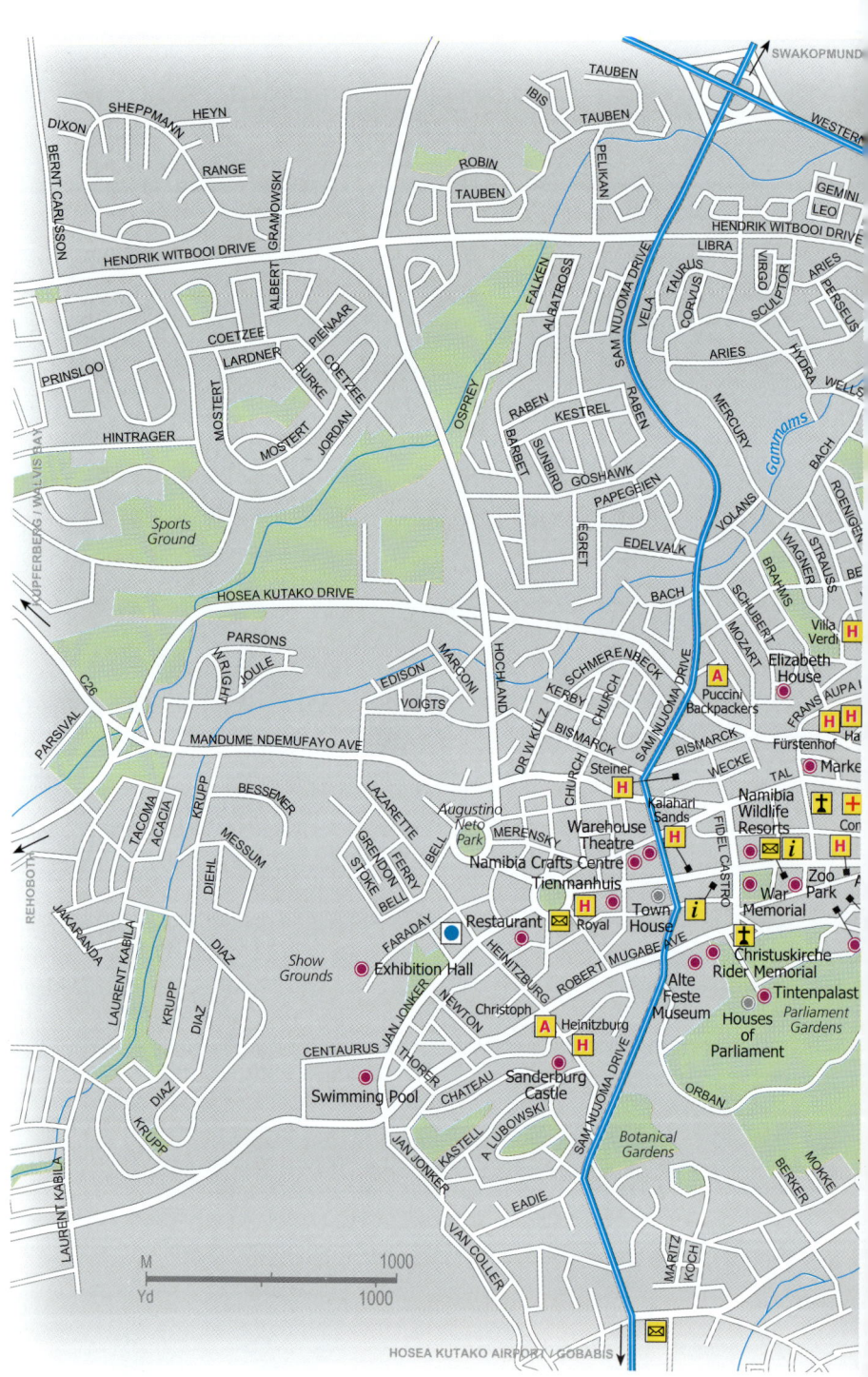

*Located 1,500m above sea level, Windhoek sits sheltered by the Eros Mountains (slightly north) and the Aus Mountains (south of the capital).*

# Windhoek Windhoek Windhoek Windh

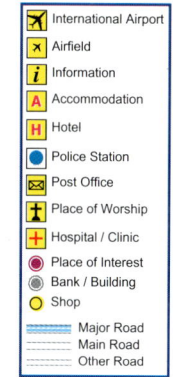

*With an average of 1mm of rain a day, Windhoek's population of just over 200,000 no doubt primarily use their umbrellas for sun protection.*

# Windhoek Windhoek Windhoek Wi

Relaxed, yet alive with people and an array of vibrant cultures, Windhoek gives the visitor a generous feeling of welcome without engulfing them like a typical western capital. Despite its large proportion of indigenous inhabitants, the concrete face of Windhoek is very German in nature, the architecture and numerous war memorials paying homage to the former colonial masters.

Windhoek has a reasonable entertainment infrastructure, with well attended and popular nightclubs, bars and restaurants. For visitors or locals seeking engagements of a more cerebral nature, there are art galleries and museums that boast impressive exhibits, as well as a theatre and a cinema (with five screens). If you're architecturally inclined you'll be able to amuse yourself for hours in Windhoek, which boasts a rich tradition of colonial German buildings in addition to newer post-modernist constructions. And, of course, the three castles on the hills (all completed by 1917) overlooking the city centre provide further fascination. Heinitzburg, the second to be built, is now an upmarket hotel and a good spot for sundowners.

WHERE THE STREETS HAVE FAMOUS NAMES
A walk down Independence Avenue will offer views of some stunning German colonial architecture, the Clock Tower, Zoo Park's lawns and palm trees, the Curt von Francois statue, and the Augustino Neto Gardens. You'll also notice some famous road names: Sam Nujoma Drive, Robert Mugabe Avenue and Nelson Mandela Drive.

THE RIDER MEMORIAL
An enormous statue stands at the entrance to the Alte Feste (Old Fort), Windhoek's oldest surviving building, and now the National Museum of Namibia. The statue – Reiter Denkmal (the Rider Memorial) – depicts a larger-than-life but typical German Protection Force soldier. The statue was erected in memory of the *Schutztruppe* (German soldiers) who died during the 1903-1907 wars against the Herero and Nama.

LOOK AT THIS
Post Street Mall boasts the largest display of meteorites in the world – or so say the locals – 33 making up a sculpture in the middle of the Mall! The Gibeon meteorites rained down on earth probably 600 million years ago, over 20 tons of rock (77 meteorites in all) having been collected in the area around Gibeon, near Mariental.

*Windhoek city walk.*

*The Rider Memorial.*

18

*In 1959 Windhoek's black population was forcibly removed to Katutura, which is Herero for "we have no dwelling place".*

# Windhoek

### ALOE-ALOE
The aloe – a hardy plant with large, fleshy leaves for storing water in arid conditions – is an icon of Namibia. Aloes usually present themselves in a stunning winter display around town, but they can also be appreciated in the Windhoek Botanical Gardens.

### DAAN VILJOEN GAME PARK
Close to Windhoek, Daan Viljoen Game Park is equipped for travellers and offers driving opportunities for standard cars. The park has three main trails: Wag-'n-Bietjie (Buffalo-thorn) Trail, Rooibos (bushwillow) Trail and Sweet-Thorn Trail. It offers good game spotting and has a prolific birdlife (including the Damara rockjumper and the rosy-faced lovebird). Walking is relatively safe as four of the Big Five (and dangerous) don't inhabit the Park (lion, elephant, rhino and buffalo).

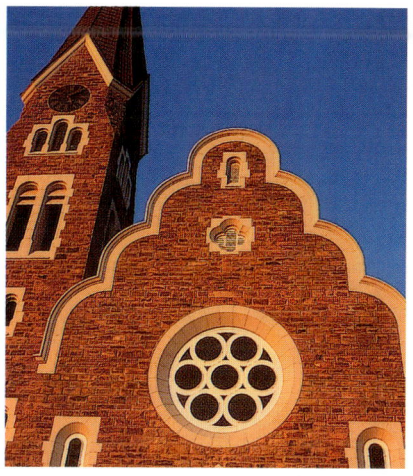

*Christuskirche, Windhoek's Evangelical Lutheran church, consecrated in 1910.*

### Top Tip
For hikers, the purchase of *Birds of Daan Viljoen* (from the parks office), will be money well spent: it has a checklist of bird species as well as other useful information on the birds and the park.

19

*Namibia's holiday mecca, Swakop (as the locals call it) offers lovely beaches for anglers, surfers, bathers and sun-worshippers to share.*

# Swakopmund Swakopmund Swak

Swakop is small enough to be explored on foot, and interesting enough to make the effort worthwhile. It's also the adventure and activity centre of Nambia (which includes parachuting, sand-boarding and dune-bike riding) and as such it's little surprise that the town is extremely tourist friendly, while maintaining the ability to slip back into sleepy-hollow mode at certain times of the week, month or year. There are plenty of cultural attractions (libraries, museums, commercial art galleries, curio stores and interesting buildings) to occupy the non-adrenaline junkie.

*Swakopmund Prison, often mistaken by visitors for a hotel.*

### Top Tip

The Sam Cohen Library has 7,000 volumes of Africana books and literature on Swakopmund, as well as old photos, maps and German and English newspapers dating back to 1898.

*English is Namibia's official language, but German is widely used ... and Swakop residents in particular are well-versed in the language.*

# Swakopmund

### RUNNING OUT OF STEAM
One of Swakop's most famous pieces of history lies just outside of town – nicknamed 'Martin Luther', the now rusty old steam engine was imported from Hamburg in Germany to take the place of oxen who struggled in the heat.

### NATIONAL MARINE AQUARIUM
Hand-feeding by divers, an underwater walkway through the huge main tank and a wide array of local marine life (ranging from sharks to crayfish) make Swakop's aquarium a good place to spend half an hour or longer.

*Swakopmund walk.*

### SWAKOP RIVER DELTA
A couple of hundred metres from the Aquarium is the Swakop River Delta, an excellent spot for birdwatching and bird photography (including flamingo, pelican, cormorants and kestrels) with a 4km river trail for walkers.

**Top Trip**
A short drive out of town are sand dunes that are ideal for adventure sports (4x4, sand dune boarding, quadbiking) as well as the Welwitschia Drive in the Namib-Naukluft Park.

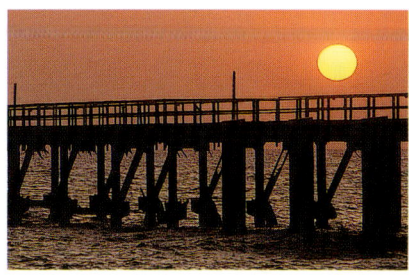

*The old jetty, originally built in 1911 during the German colonial era.*

### THE ABOMINABLE JETTY
Swakop's well-known iron jetty stretches 262m into the ocean but is now unfortunately dilapidated, has been closed to the public and exists merely as a landmark rather than a tourist 'attraction'. The lighthouse can be seen from as far as 30km away – a good thing considering how treacherous Namibia's Skeleton Coast has been over the last century.

### HARBOURING NO BAD FEELINGS
Swakop was founded by the Germans in 1892 in order to match the British who had already established their own 'port presence' at Walvis Bay on the strategically valuable Skeleton Coast. Sadly, Swakop proved a poor choice, as the harbour was prone to silting up. Just 14 years later the government hoped the construction of a mole would help to create an artificial harbour that could function properly. Regrettably, sandbanks built up and ruined any chance for the harbour. On a more positive note, it did improve the safety and bathing pleasure for beach users and the mole is now used as a launching spot for boats and small craft. It also allows walkers the chance to see dolphins at close range.

*Swakopmund is a good base for visiting the dramatic Spitzkoppe, which are just over 100km away from town.*

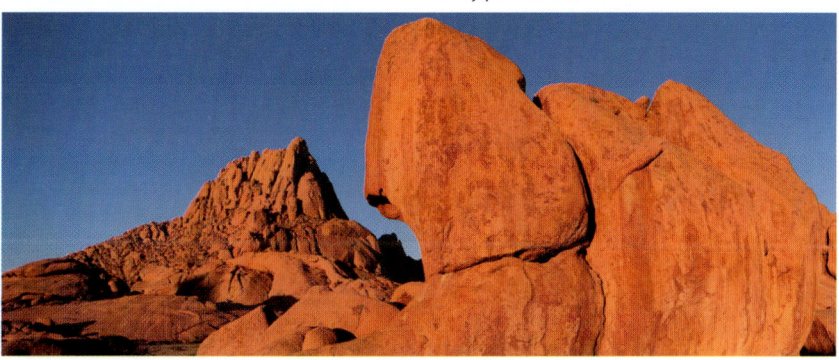

*Walvis Bay's huge saltwater lagoon is a vital habitat for flamingoes who flock there in their thousands all year round.*

# Walvis Bay Walvis Bay Walvis Bay

The long, straight and rolling road between Walvis Bay and Swakopmund.

*Namibia's best natural harbour (and only deepwater port), Walvis is a vital base for patrolling the valuable fishing ground and offshore diamond fields.*

# Walvis Bay Walvis Bay Walvis Bay

Walvis Bay lies 30km south of Swakopmund, and many visitors stay in Swakop and journey down to Walvis to partake in the birdwatching (numerous seabirds, including the favourite flamingoes and pelicans), angling, seal-spotting cruises offshore (if you're in luck you'll get to see dolphin and even sunfish from your craft), or the more leisurely boating activities on the lagoon. The architecture of the town lacks the character of Swakop's German charm, possibly because the port was annexed by the British in 1878 (the Germans never took control of Walvis and were forced to lay port elsewhere).

### Top Trip

**Avoid the tourist trap of activities centred solely on the lagoon – explore some of the magnificent desert sights and scenery that surrounds the town. It's an experience largely untapped by visitors.**

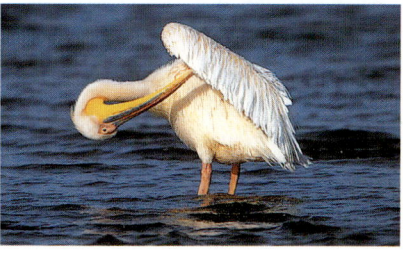

*Top: Greater flamingoes in flight.*
*Above: Pelican preening itself.*

The legendary Bartolomeu Dias is down in the history books as the first European to visit here, back in 1487, and he named the spot Bay of Whales. For the next two centuries whalers and numerous other vessels dropped anchor in Walvis Bay (as well as at Sandwich Harbour), and when the Dutch came to town in 1793 they adapted its name to Walvisbaai (Walvis Bay), and some claim their influence is still felt in the town's lack of architectural character! Walvis' small population of just over 40,000 rely on fish and fishing for their livelihood as well as salt production (Walvis supplies more than 90% of South Africa's salt). The salt is evaporated from seawater trapped in a 3,500-hectare 'salt pan'. Tours of the salt works are offered by local tour operators. Walvis Bay Lagoon is one of the two most valuable wetland areas (along with the nearby Sandwich Harbour) to be found throughout the entire West coast of Africa. The lagoon is able to support more than 150,000 birds in summer and almost 70,000 in winter, notably the greater and lesser flamingoes, pelicans, migrant waders and seabirds. Wait for low-tide to get your best birding opportunities as the birds scour the shallow water for tasty marine morsels.

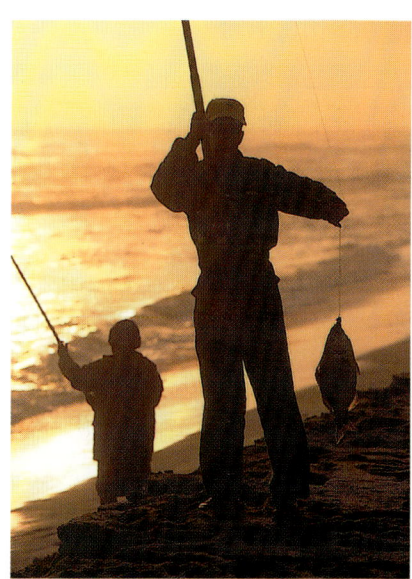

*A good catch, a quiet beach, and a friend to bear witness to your success. Fisherman's paradise!*

### Top Tip

**For a different experience, stop by the Raft Restaurant (built on stilts in the Walvis Bay lagoon) and enjoy a bite to eat or a drink at the bar. It's 'a good place to be seen'!**

*The unusual pastel shades of many of the houses in this laid-back but character-rich town have led some to playfully call it 'Ludicrous'.*

# Lüderitz Lüderitz Lüderitz Lüderitz

**Top Tip**

Plan your wardrobe carefully: Lüderitz's weather is 'predictably unpredictable'. Within a few hours Mother Nature might hurl sunshine, fog, cold, wind and even rain at you. Locals 'joke' that the wind is so strong it blasts the paint off cars. Joke?

*Some of Lüderitz's brightly coloured buildings.*

A favourite travel destination and a stunning example of friendly, small-town and slow-paced hospitality, rich in German tradition and history, Lüderitz is worth the effort to visit for a few days. Sitting more than 360km from Keetmanshoop, Lüderitz is literally and figuratively isolated from the rest of the world. However, it's not cut off completely, as it has a rich supply of public telephones that seem to pop up on every corner. Tourism is increasing and accommodation options are happily opening up to meet the new demand, with the first phase of a new waterfront development already completed. Part of Lüderitz's charm is that its isolation for so many years has left the town with a wealth of original architecture and interesting buildings from the 1900s. Added to this is the fun nature of the town, with its eccentric house colours and the midday siren that doubles-up as a fire alarm! Bartolomeu Dias also made his mark here and named the town Angra Pequena (Little Bay). A number of tools and artefacts dating back to the stone-age confirm that the Khoisan found 'Little Bay' some time before Dias! Kolmanskop and Elizabeth Bay ghost towns are a comfortable drive from Lüderitz and are both worth the effort.

*Named after the six springs (ses fontein) found here, this dusty little town in the middle of nowhere lies central to all the delights of northwest Namibia.*

# esfontein Opuwo Sesfontein Opuw

### SESFONTEIN ▼

Fort Sesfontein was established as a German army outpost to keep an eye on the area militarily as well as from a crime and gun-running perspective prior to World War I. Abandoned and in an awful state of deterioration for decades, it was given a facelift and general overhaul and converted into a comfy oasis-like lodge. It's an ideal base for explorations into the surrounding Kaokoland and Damaraland. The historic graveyard is worth a wander. Take in the views of the town and its mountain backdrop from the shale and limestone hills that skirt the fort.

*A wall of tins built by the locals in Opuwo.*

Opuwo made its name as a base used by the South African troops during times of conflict and occupation in Namibia. It is an otherwise unpretentious little settlement lost in the bush and tucked away in its own small 'crater', although there are some interesting local dwellings, such as traditional rondavels (round huts) and Himba huts. Opuwo has two 'supermarkets' and a fish shop called Madiba (Nelson Mandela's nickname).

About 29km out of town is Ongongo Camp, which means 'beautiful little place', and the Blinkwater Falls back up this claim. Otjitaimo Canyon is 10km out of town and is hard to reach on foot, yet it offers rich rewards for seekers of solitude and spectacular scenery.

**Top Tip**
Locals will be willing to act as guides to the town (for a fee), but they no longer think tourist cameras are worth a free smile. Be careful when encroaching on tribal land and always seek permission.

**Top Trip**
A day trip along the **Hoanib River** from Sesfontein to Purros offers great viewing of the desert elephant as well as numerous other forms of wildlife. Please note that it is advisable to travel with a guide.

### OPUWO ▶

Opuwo means 'the end' in the native Herero tongue, which is fitting as it is a vital stocking-up point for travellers passing through ... and passing through is what most people do in Opuwo, apart from using it as a base for exploring the surrounding area, which includes some nearby settlements of Himba and Herero people. Kaokoveld adventurers and explorers often use Opuwo as a stop-off point, or stop relatively near by.

25

*Rundu presents weary Caprivi-bound travellers with a relative oasis to wash away the bleak desert landscape through which they have travelled.*

# Oshakati Rundu Oshakati Rundu

### OSHAKATI
Big and spread out, Oshakati is primarily a residential and governmental town, hosting the Northern Campus of the University of Namibia, some private schools and municipal buildings. There are many comfortable homes in town, but there equally areas which offer more basic housing and services.

### RUNDU
Situated above the Kavango (Okavango in Botswana) River floodplain, Rundu is a fabulous stopover en route to more entertaining and enjoyable activities or destinations, in the Kavango and Caprivi regions. Its proximity to Angola has given the little outpost of Rundu a Portuguese flavour mixed with a languid sense of calm. There are great views across the Kavango River, with some watersports, fishing and four-wheel drive opportunities for the energetic. Rundu is an important refueling stop for travellers: petrol is scarce in the area, and the town's bottle stores present shoppers with a fantastic array of products. Souvenir hunters will enjoy Rundu's happy hunting grounds: woodcarving in the area has a proud tradition.

**Top Tip:** Oshakati offers the potential of a big night out in a small town. Basic but welcoming, favourite spots include Club Fantasy (proclaiming itself to be 'your party place'), Let's Push Bar, Club Yellow Star and Moby Jack's.

*Woodcarvings for sale in Rundu.*

26

*The patron saint of mine workers (believe it or not) is St Barbara ... and you'll find Tsumeb's St Barbara catholic church on Main Street.*

# atima Mulilo Tsumeb Tsumeb Katin

*The mokoro (dug-out), a popular means of transport in the wetlands.*

### KATIMA MULILO ▲
Katima Mulilo boasts excellent facilities for travellers and is a great base for exploring as well as embarking on adventure activities. Located on the banks of the mighty Zambezi River, it provides an easy base from which to hop into Zambia, Zimbabwe or Botswana.

### TSUMEB ▼
Tsumeb is attractive, with wide, quiet streets blessed with beautiful old colonial buildings and dressed with jacaranda, bougainvillea, palm trees, parks and lawns. Tsumeb's name can be translated to mean 'to dig a hole in loose ground', which is understandable given its status as one of Namibia's key mining towns. The crystals and gemstones unearthed here have earned the town a worldwide reputation. The Tsumeb Museum affords visitors a fantastic window into the past, while the Tsumeb Cultural Village is an open-air museum that allows visitors to glimpse first-hand what tribal life is all about in Namibia.

### Top Sip
It's rough and ready for most big city folk; local eateries include The Butchy-Butchy Bakery (offering freshly baked bread) or you can rub shoulders with the local Crocodile Dundees at Mad Dog McGee's (a meat-eater's haven).

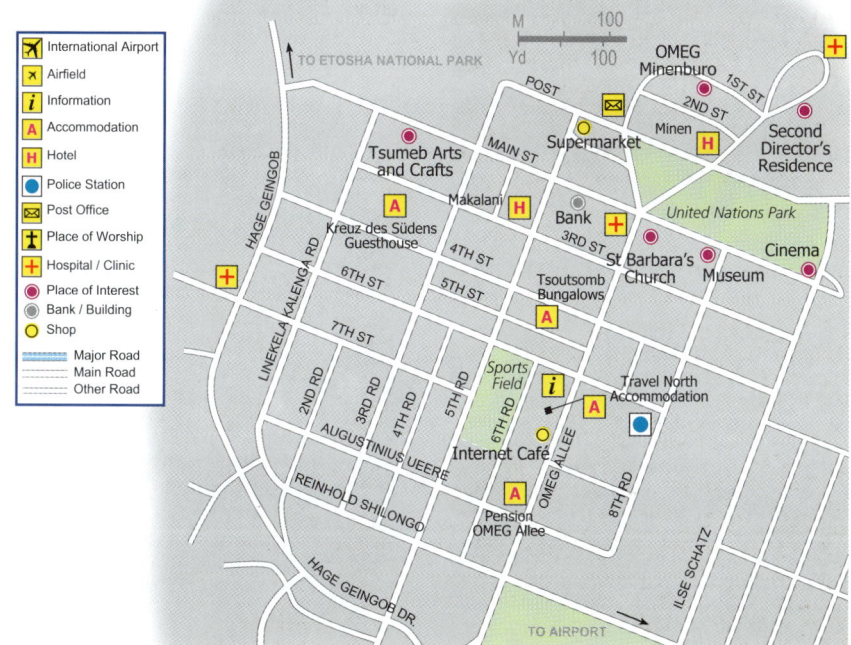

27

*Otavi, Grootfontein and Tsumeb form the Maize Triangle, cultivating and providing much of Namibia's commercially grown maize.*

# Grootfontein Otavi Otavi Grootfon

### GROOTFONTEIN ▼
Meaning 'large fountain' (there are strong natural springs in Tree Park), Grootfontein offers a pleasant stopover, as trees line the streets and limestone buildings stand proudly amid the spring explosions of jacaranda and red flamboyants.

**Top Tip:** A 2km drive out of Otavi will bring you to the Khorab Memorial. Erected in 1920, it marks the spot where the German forces capitulated to General Louis Botha's South African forces in 1915.

*The enormous Hoba meteorite that landed near Grootfontein many thousands of years ago.*

### OTAVI ▼
Otavi's natural springs play a vital role in irrigating the surrounding farmlands, and it's no surprise that the name translates to 'place of water'. The town made its name during the copper-mining boom years at the turn of the century, and an amethyst mine is found just out of town.

Otavi hit the headlines with the 1991 discovery of the jawbone of a prehistoric ape-like creature dubbed the 'Otavi Ape', a creature which no doubt spent some time in the abundant caves in the area – anyone with an interest in caves will enjoy a great deal of time 'caving' themselves.

The fascinating Old Fort Museum (signposted as Die Alte Feste) off Eriksson Street has interesting historic photographs, gems, rocks and a display on the old art of wagon and cart manufacture. Straussen Ostrich Farm offers an insight into the ostrich industry, and includes a shop and a restaurant. The Hoba meteorite – the largest recorded meteorite on earth at around 60 tonnes – can be found 50km outside town. Almost three metres square (and between 75-122cm thick!), it may have celebrated in the region of 200 to 400 million birthdays, and it found its home here around 80,000 years ago.

28

*Outjo means (appropriately) 'a place on the rocks', while Otjiwarongo was named by the Herero who thought of it as the 'place of the fat cattle'.*

# Outjo Otjiwarongo Otjiwarongo Ou

### Top Trip
An hour or so outside of Otjiwarongo are a number of fossilised footprints that date back 200 million years! Stare in awe at the massive set of prints made by a very large two-legged dinosaur.

### OTJIWARONGO ▲
Known for its spring explosions of jacaranda and bougainvillea, Otjiwarongo is situated close to the Waterberg Plateau Park. Otjiwarongo boasts Namibia's first crocodile ranch, which serves meals to visitors, sells meat to locals and exports skins to Asia. Just out of town on the road to Otavi is an 18-hole golf course watched over by the dramatic granite rock formation they call 'Whale Rock'. Look out for the famous Locomotive No 41 at the train station ... but don't rush to catch it! Since 1960 it hasn't gone anywhere as the railway gauge was changed from narrow to 1.067mm gauge. No 41 is now a luxury hotel ... and a trainspotters' delight!

### OUTJO ▼
Outjo revolves around cattle-ranching and one-night stay tourists en route to Etosha National Park, Khorixas or northern Kaokoland. One of the town's most outstanding (literally) landmarks is the Water Tower, which has stood tall since 1901. The town museum is in Franke House, which dates back to 1899 and was one of Outjo's first homes. The museum shows off a wide range of minerals and gemstones, local history artifacts, and numerous animal skins, bones and horns ... and has a one-of-a-kind sheep-sheering device that operates off a bicycle chain! The nearby Ugab Terrace hills offer spectacular rock formations, including middle age castle shapes. Gamkarab Cave (50km away) boasts stalagmites and -tites of distinction.

*Omaruru's name is derived from a somewhat unfortunate Herero description of cattle milk, omaere omruru, or bitter curd.*

# Omaruru Omaruru Henties Bay Her

### OMARURU ▲
A dry river (most of the year) runs through the surprisingly green and pretty town of Omaruru. The major attraction in town is Franke Tower, which proudly commemorates the German captain who helped to repel the Hereros in 1904. More of the town's early history can be viewed in the museum at Mission House, Omaruru's oldest building. On the outskirts of town is the Kristall Kellerei (kellerei means 'cellars'), Namibia's first winery. Omaruru and its surroundings offer good birding opportunities, especially the possibility of ticking off some of the north-western endemics. Several game lodges in the area (which offer luxury accommodation) have been stocked with a wide variety of antelope, giraffe and rhino. The Erongo Massif near Omaruru is an excellent spot for rock climbers.

### HENTIES BAY ▼
Hentie van der Merwe first started fishing here in 1929, and little did he know that a town would grow here and adopt his name. A sleepy hollow, Henties wakes up for the summer season to welcome the 10,000-plus visitors who flock to this fisherman's paradise, many with an eye on casting a line into the ocean or swinging their clubs at the 9-hole golf course that runs through a valley down towards the beach. The town has plenty of petrol stations to cater for the lack of supply further north.

*Cape Fur Seals line the rocks and sand at Cape Cross, 60km north of Henties Bay.*

*Okahandja is renowned for offering some of the best fresh vegetables in Namibia, while Gobabis produces a third of the country's red meat.*

# Gobabis Gobabis Okahandja Okahar

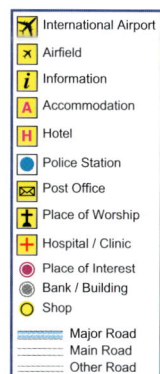

## GOBABIS ▲
Gobabis has a special charm for passing tourists on this vital route through to Botswana. There are pretty old church buildings in town and a golf course. A statue of a bull at the town's western entrance bears testament to the importance of cattle to the Omaheke region, which has the second-highest number of cattle in all of Namibia's 13 regions.

### Top Tip
The old experimental tobacco station in Okhandja is a photogenic building. It was started up in 1906 and hoped to capitalize on planting tobacco and rolling out cigars. Operations have long since ceased and the building is now empty and overgrown.

### Top Trip
The farms around Gobabis offer game drives, but keep your eye out for the splendid sight of the local Herero women dressed in their traditional costumes.

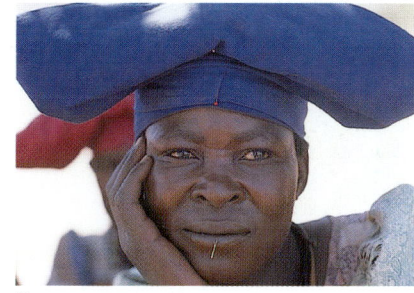

*Herero woman.*

## ◀ OKAHANDJA
Okahandja might be small, but it boasts some of Namibia's finest open-air markets specializing in souvenirs such as wood-carvings (notably enormous hippos, huge giraffe and up to 2m tall human busts) as well as art from all around Namibia, Zimbabwe and even central Africa. The administrative 'capital' of the Herero, Okahandja hosts a large and colourful annual festival in August to honour the Herero forefathers. Okahandja is set in excellent farming country. There are numerous historic sights in and around town, including Moordkoppie (Murder Hill, the scene of the 1850 Herero massacre) and many graves of influential local leaders from the last 100 years (including that of the Oorlam leader Jan Jonker Afrikaner).

*Rehoboth's hot springs were called Anhes (smoke) by the Swartbooi Namas because of the steam that rises from the hot water.*

# Mariental Mariental Rehoboth

### REHOBOTH ▶
You have to see the Rehoboth museum (built in 1903, and found behind the post office) ... partly because there are few other attractions in town. Aside from a fascinating collection and display of bank notes and various items of local history, flora and fauna, you'll find a good history of the proud Baster people for whom Rehoboth is now their cultural home.

### MARIENTAL ▼
Forget about peace and tranquility here: Mariental suffers from an unhappy climate. The heat is atrocious in summer, the cold is biting in winter, and the changes in season bring strong winds that blow dust everywhere. Local industry focusses on cultivating animal fodder, fruit and vegetables, as well as ostrich meat and karakul pelts, aided by its proximity to the Hardap Dam (Namibia's largest reservoir). Hardap itself is enjoyed by anglers, hikers, birders and boating enthusiasts. The town owes its name to Herman Brandt, the first colonial settler in the area, who made his wife happy by naming it Marie's Valley (hence Mariental).

**Top Tip:** Rehoboth's spa offers a pleasant hot spring enjoyed by the Nama for centuries, though now somewhat the worse for wear. Oanob Lake Resort is becoming increasingly popular for watersports, hiking and birdwatching.

*The hub of the Karakul wool industry, Keetmanshoop is the 'capital of the south' and its road junction links Lüderitz, South Africa and Windhoek.*

# eetmanshoop Keetmanshoop Keet

Keetmanshoop (shortened to 'Keet' by the locals) is a sunny town with attractive German colonial architecture, pretty gardens and a rustic museum. 'Keet' is situated almost 500km south of Windhoek and roughly 1,000m above sea level. The original church was built in 1866 but, alas, 24 years later a freak flood washed the entire building away! Its replacement (the current town museum) was put up five years later ... this time on somewhat higher ground!

*Keetmanshoop museum.*

33

# Key Touring Maps Key Touring M

Namibia represents an uneasy compromise between man and nature to carve out their territory of choice. Jagged and – in places – treacherous natural borders were created by centuries of persistent erosion by the mighty Atlantic Ocean, while the top and bottom of this vast land have been chipped away by great rivers with memories deeper than humankind: the Orange, Cunene, Kavango, Zambezi and Chobe. Where nature failed to penetrate the remaining borders, man stepped in to rule straight lines of territorial control. This strange shape for such a stark yet hauntingly beautiful land befits a country that has seen much pain and suffering. It's as though someone had tried to tame the land, but nature reminds travellers and settlers that it can't be harnessed, can't be approached lightly or without caution. It allows man to take dangerous liberties as his pride and courage urge him to conquer the elements.
Yet always Namibia will win.
This is a land which is a great ally, but an even greater enemy.

Etosha ('great white place' in Herero, due to the bright sun) is one of the finest game reserves to be found in Southern Africa.

# Etosha Etosha Etosha Etosha Etos

Etosha is a vital game reserve for the entire Southern Africa region and is home to 114 species of mammal, 340 bird species, 110 different reptiles, 16 species of amphibians and yet just one fish species. All this is found in the 22,000km² that makes up the park named after the massive pan that covers a vast 5,000km², stretching roughly 120km from east to west and some 70km across at its widest point. The pan seldom boasts much water (if any) as it is fed by the rains rather than reliable rivers, and even when the rains fall hard few areas fill up or flood due to the incredibly high rate of evaporation. The rainy season signals the arrival of summer migrants in the form of

*Oryx (or gemsbok) tend to congregate around Etosha's waterholes.*

36

*Etosha is best explored in your own car without a guide. The roads are good and the open landscape allows for excellent wildlife spotting.*

# Etosha Etosha Etosha Etosha Etos

mammals and birds. In good years the pan will be alive with thousands of flamingoes. The western reaches of Etosha feature some unique areas, including the fascinating Moringa Forest or Haunted Forest (dubbed *Sprokieswoud* in Afrikaans) with its weirdly contorted moringa trees – possibly shaped by browsing herds of elephant and giraffe. Etosha has three main rest camps (Namutoni, Halali and Okaukuejo) with perimeter fencing and superb floodlit waterholes which are open 24 hours a day. The world's largest game reserve until the 1960s, when its surface area was reduced by nearly 80%, Etosha remains one of the largest and most important parks in Africa.

*A lioness defending her territory. She also has to do the bulk of the hunting to feed the pride.*

## Top Tip

It is possible to use your own 2WD vehicle in Etosha for transport and animal-watching. There's no need to hire a 4WD vehicle, and organized tours are not essential to your enjoyment of what the park has to offer.

37

The name Naukluft means 'narrow ravine'. This dramatic landscape is much loved by hikers, four-wheel drive enthusiasts and photographers alike.

## Sossusvlei Namib-Naukluft Sossus

Larger than Switzerland, the 50,000km²-plus of fantastically scenic desert landscape occupied by the Namib-Naukluft Park ranks it with the biggest in all of Africa. It represents a vital conservation effort to retain the pristine nature of the Namib desert, which vies with the Atacama Desert in South America for the title of oldest on earth. You'll need plenty of time to enjoy all that the park has to offer, so keep your itinerary flexible. The Namib has an amazing array of wildlife, with many plants found in the mountainous region, an area enjoyed by the rare Hartmann's mountain zebra as well as leopards and other shy animals who appreciate the vegetation and sanctuary offered by the many caves, gorges and rocky terrain. There are also numerous small nocturnal delights (insects and reptiles) to be found throughout the area, while birdwatchers will delight in the bustling air traffic around the deep kloof which has water throughout the year. Horse-riding and hiking are popular ways to traverse much of this region, with hikes ranging from a few hours up to the more advanced eight-day, 120km Naukluft Hiking Trail.

*Sossusvlei's Dead Pan is surrounded by dunes and filled with long-dead trees.*

*Sesriem Canyon derives its name from* ses riem *(six thongs), the number of rope lengths needed to draw water from the 30m deep gorge.*

## Namib-Naukluft Sossusvlei

Sossusvlei, with its stark yet striking beauty, is one of the natural world's great photo opportunities. The occasional rain quickly sinks into the thirsty ground – it sustains hardy camel thorn acacias and the indestructible *!nara*, a melon-bearing plant that offers vital nourishment to a variety of animals in this unforgiving territory. The skeletal remains of ancient trees in Dead Vlei (some of which lived centuries ago) are all that remains of easier times, when rain was more plentiful and sustained a variety of flora. Lovers of sand and dunes will be in their element at Sossusvlei as the vlei (pan) is surrounded by one of the world's tallest sand dunes. These can rise 300m and are best viewed as the early morning sun breaks the horizon, highlighting the redness of the sand. The sand at Sesriem (which acts as the gateway to Sossusvlei) is ocean sand blown inland. A number of camps, lodges and campsites allow visitors quick access (by foot, 4WD or shuttle) to this dramatic landscape with its great walking opportunities and fascinating geological formations.

*Sossusvlei's glowing red dunes.*

39

> Kaokoland is rugged and remote. Entrusting your travel arrangements to someone who does not know it intimately is simply asking for trouble.

# Kaokoland Kaokoland Kaokoland

The Kaokoland presents one of Namibia's greatest challenges: a vast stretch of land that is alluring yet utterly inhospitable to all but the local Himbas and extremely well-prepared travellers. Located in north-west Namibia, Kaokoland is an extremely barren mountain desert region, offering little in the way of water or vegetation, yet despite its desolation it displays a unique beauty. Its floral delights are spectacular, bottle trees rising from rocky *koppies* (hills) boldly defying the elements. Look closely and tread carefully and you will discover a wide range of succulents underfoot. Animals are scarce, the legacy of unscrupulous hunting, poaching and the unfortunate large-scale slaughter of wildlife for food during the desperate struggle for independence. If you're in luck you'll come across cheetah, leopard and lion, or some of the small herds of springbok and gemsbok, in addition to zebra and giraffe. The area is perhaps more famed for the presence of black rhino (Kaokoland is the black rhino's last free-roaming area on earth) and the desert elephant. These hardy elephants have extra-long legs to help them trudge the barren land, up to 70km a day, looking for nourishment. They can survive

| GPS 1 | GPS 6 | GPS 11 |
|---|---|---|
| 17°14'50"S 12°25'09"E | 17°37'25"S 12°51'29"E | 17°46'56"S 12°57'43"E |
| GPS 2 | GPS 7 | GPS 12 |
| 17°33'18"S 12°33'14"E | 17°28'04"S 13°03'41"E | 17°51'45"S 13°01'26"E |
| GPS 3 | GPS 8 | GPS 13 |
| 17°47'23"S 12°23'20"E | 17°13'40"S 13°14'11"E | 18°03'29"S 13°15'31"E |
| GPS 4 | GPS 9 | GPS 14 |
| 17°47'49"S 12°31'22"E | 17°26'01"S 13°16'20"E | 18°04'18"S 12°44'29"E |
| GPS 5 | GPS 10 | GPS 15 |
| 17°39'20"S 12°41'43"E | 17°20'28"S 13°50'56"E | 18°09'22"S 12°33'38"E |

*The Kaokoland's terrain might be tough and unforgiving, but it remains fragile: some tyre tracks made decades earlier remain to this day.*

# Kaokoland Kaokoland Kaokoland Kao

for up to five days without water. The area is dangerous for travellers, as the searing heat and barren environment offer little sustenance for those trapped without transport, roads often get washed away in the rain, while dry riverbeds have quicksand spots that have been known to swallow vehicles. Travellers should not consider tackling this harsh territory without at least one other vehicle in tow, an experienced navigator and meticulous planning and preparation. Aside from personal safety, be extremely sensitive to the environment when driving overland. There are numerous rough paths, but make sure that you always stick to existing tracks as this will limit the damage to vegetation and animals. Try to avoid unnecessary driving or joy-riding over sandy areas in particular. Flanked by baobabs on either side, the Cunene River to the north offers a wide range of water-based diversions to cater for all tastes and levels of courage and skill.

## Top Tip

The Cunene River boasts numerous water-sport opportunities to cater for mild to wild interests. The surrounding vegetation (lush by Kaokoland standards!) acts like a magnet for wildlife and tourists alike.

*Kaokoland's varying landscapes.*

41

*Loch Ness has nothing on the Fish River Canyon: local legend claims that the mighty meanders in the canyon were caused by a massive snake!*

# Fish River Canyon

One of Africa's great natural wonders (and one of the world's largest canyons, behind America's Grand Canyon), the Fish River Canyon provides an awesome spectacle as well as an abundance of adventure activities. The canyon itself is massive, 500m deep and over 25km wide in some places, and stretching a distance of around 160km. Part of the Ai-Ais conservation area, the canyon lies near Namibia's southern border, offering easy access from South Africa. The Ai-Ais rest camp, on the banks of the Fish River, accommodates most of the canyon's visitors. It is located near the hot springs in the canyon (Ai-Ais means very hot in the Nama tongue) and is surrounded by dramatic lunar-like landscape.

It is possible to visit the canyon without spending a night in Ai-Ais (if your budget or schedule is tight), as day-trips can be made from Keetmanshoop and other nearby bases. This will, however, limit the time available to explore the canyon and indulge in all the acitivities offered by lodges and rest camps in the area: horse-riding, day hikes (with or without a guide), overnight hikes and camping (such as at Hobas, which is close to the canyon's main viewpoint), driving trips, animal- and bird-watching, or simple walks to the viewing spots to enjoy the unforgettable vistas. The ultimate experience is a flight over the canyon with views that go on forever – a memory that will last a lifetime. The canyon contains deposits of sandstone, shale and lava millions of years old. The geology around the Canyon, and along its seemingly endless course, is fascinating, with scores of amazing rock formations, intrusive granites and dolerite dykes.

Forming the natural border between South Africa and Namibia, the Orange (or Gariep) River offers a variety of water adventures, from gently drifting down the river from one riverside camp to the next, to adrenaline-pumping white-water bashes over rocks and rapids that can challenge (and terrify) even the most experienced rivermen. River trips generally range from four to six days and can be combined with a five-day horseback trail if you have any energy and nerve left.

**Right:** *The tiny klipspringer (half a metre at the shoulder) can elude any predator ... so long as the chase is over rocky terrain.*
**Below:** *A view from the bottom of the canyon.*

*The popular Ai-Ais hot springs oasis on the banks of the Fish River has experienced temperatures of 47°C.*

# Fish River Canyon

43

!Nara *melons, endemic to the Namib desert, are a valuable food source for desert scavengers as well as a traditional food of the Topnaar Namas.*

# Namib-Naukluft Park & West Coast

Previously known as the Namib Desert Park, the Namib section of the Namib-Naukluft Park (Africa's third-largest nature reserve, Park) offers plenty of worthwhile attractions, including the majestic cliffs and ravines of the Kuiseb Canyon, with plenty of overnight and four-wheel drive opportunities. Widely regarded as the oldest desert on earth, it is believed that the Namib Desert has 'enjoyed' its arid to semi-arid conditions for as long as 80 million years. The West Coast offers fantastic hiking and driving trips (especially along the Skeleton Coast), as well as excellent fishing. A treacherous coastline over the centuries, many ships have run aground here. It's harshness is typified in the landmark Bogenfels Arch which is, unfortunately, no longer accessible to the public.

*The dramatic Bogenfels Arch, a 50m-high rock arch south of Lüderitz on the West Coast.*

44

*The wetlands at Sandwich Harbour offer a haven for birds, and the unspoilt coastline and spectacular scenery make it a popular tourist stop.*

# Namib-Naukluft Park & West Coast

*Four-wheel drive trips along the Skeleton Coast offer a unique driving experience, yet it demands caution and a large degree of consideration for the environment.*

45

*Driving in two-vehicle (at least) convoys in Mamili National Park is strongly advised ... regardless of your perceived survival skills.*

# Mamili Mamili Mamili Mamili Mam

The 32,000ha Mamili National Park was opened at the same time as Mudumu (1990), and they act as the eastern Caprivi's only protected areas. The Linyandi Swamp are a major drawcard when the Kwando River is running full (often flooding around June), which provides lazy mokoro (dugout) trips to explore the forested islands, wetlands and reeded channels. Naturally, there is abundant birdlife (more than 430 species) in addition to other wildlife (from elephant to lion, giraffe and hippo, along with numerous buck), despite the past ravages of poachers' weapons. Mokoro and 4WD are the only way to get around Mamili. This is not the place to take personal risks, as help can be a long time coming. There are rangers on patrol throughout the park, but they might not cross your path in time if you've found your way into a spot of difficulty. Gameviewing is best before the rainy season, which can start as early as October. The best birding opportunities are between December and March when the migrants move in, but then the 'black cotton' clay (road) tracks could become totally inaccessible.

*The African jacana has unusually long toes which are well adapted for the wetland environments it frequents: the long toes allow it to walk and even run on floating plants without sinking.*

**Top Tip**
Camps indicated have no facilities and are merely designated spots.

*Mamili National Park Proposed name change to Rupara National Park*

> Mudumu was renowned as Namibia's greatest wildlife habitat before the ravages of poaching took their toll, but the park remains alive with fauna.

# Mudumu Mudumu Mudumu Mudum

Spread across 100,000ha, Mudumu is hugged to the west by the Kwando River, which is alive with crocodile, hippo and numerous water-loving buck (sitatunga, red lechwe and reedbuck). Covered in mopane woodlands, the reserve is well-populated with elephant, giraffe and zebra, in addition to impala, kudu, red lechwe and the somewhat uncommon roan antelope species. These animals enjoy the shelter and foliage offered by the abundant mopane. Bird-watchers will fall in love with Mudumu, especially if they get to spot the African Fish Eagle, the Narina trogon, Pel's fishing owl, or any of the many species found nowhere else in Namibia. It's best to explore Mudumu by 4WD, but Lianshulu Lodge and Lianshulu Bush Lodge offer guided walks. For a cultural diversion, visit the Lizauli Traditional Village just outside Mudumu to learn about traditional Caprivi lifestyles (from food to farming methods, medicine to crafts and toolmaking). Lizauli

*Burchell's zebra enjoy the mopane-rich environment of the Mudumu National Park.*

is one of many local upliftment programmes and is worth supporting if you are environmentally or culturally sensitive.

47

*Khaudum is wild, four-wheel drive country. Its remoteness might add to its charm, but it demands travelling in a group with adequate supplies.*

# Khaudum Game Reserve

The lack of fencing around Khaudum (with the exception of the boundary with Botswana) allows animals to leave the park in search of fresh grazing and water during the rainy season, thus ensuring an abundance of wildlife to enjoy, particularly wild dogs and roan antelope. Game viewing is best in winter, as long as you have patience and discipline: these free-roaming animals don't take kindly to noise, particularly from humans and their vehicles! The artificial waterholes provide some of the best wildlife spotting. Heavier summer rain thickens the dry woodland savannah (located on settled parts of the Kalahari's sand dunes), which encourages an abundance of birdlife for 'twitchers' to enjoy.

*Sunset in the Khaudum Game Reserve.*

*The Waterberg Plateau is centred totally on the animals and their needs. Tourists may not drive themselves around and must fit in with the animals.*

# Vaterberg Plateau Park Waterberg

The Waterberg Plateau dominates the surrounding landscape, its steep cliffs rise hundreds of metres above the surrounding plains, making the plateau a safe haven for wildlife. Many of Namibia's endangered species have been rehomed here to protect them from poachers and predators alike. This animal paradise towers a breathtaking 1,800m-plus above sea level and, aided by an amazing biodiversity which enables this small park to support a wide array of animals, it is a conservation success that actually supplies rare species of game and wildlife to many of Namibia's other parks. You can drive around the park on one of the limited, organized game drive ... but NOT on your own. The animals prefer it that way! Walking in the park provides incredible scenery and game viewing opportunities. The attractions include more than 200 species of birds (with black eagles and Cape vultures), as well as age-old dinosaur tracks and numerous examples of San rock art.

*A natural still life in the Waterberg.*

### Top Tip
The three-day (guided) Waterberg Wilderness Trail covers 10-15km a day with no set route.

49

Hardap Dam's capacity amounts to 323 million cubic meters of water held by a 39m-high, 865m-long dam wall, and offering a surface area of 25km².

# Hardap Hardap Lüderitz Peninsula

#### LÜDERITZ PENINSULA
A trip around the peninsula (in calm weather) will offer up some fabulous views and swimming possibilities at one of the many bays along the coast (Dias Point and Griffith Bay offer stunning views), while the rusted remnants of Sturmvogel Bucht's 'deceased' Norwegian Whaling Station is worth a look.

#### HARDAP GAME RESERVE
Hardap covers 23,420ha and offers driving trails as well as excellent predator-free walking trails, especially around Crater Hills (named for the rough terrain it encloses). The birdlife is superb thanks to the large dam, with over 250 species spotted here, including the majestic African Fish Eagle.

*Most of Kolmanskop's buildings remain as they were 40 years ago when its inhabitants left, leaving the desert sand to invade.*

# Kolmanskop Kolmanskop Kolmans

*The ghostly interior of a Kolmanskop house.*

The desert ghost-town of Kolmanskop is accessible for visitors, lying just 10km from Lüderitz. The diamond boom saw this town spring up in 1908 and become the centre of the region's diamond industry. During its boom years the streets and businesses bustled with determined prospectors, stars in their eyes, readily diving into the desert's sands in search of their fortunes. Its attraction now is as a tourist stop to explore the sand-ravaged ghost town, 'dead' for over 40 years ... so you won't be able to enjoy the town's former facilities of an ice factory, casino and excellent theatre, although the skittle alley has been restored to working order.

**Top Tip**
Be sure to organize your special sunrise and sunset permit, otherwise no pictures!

51

**Touring/Driving Maps** Touring/Driv

## Touring/Driving Maps

Namibia's long, straight roads demand from travellers time, patience and endurance as they draw you vast distances between the country's many cultural attractions, which range from colonial outposts and strongholds through to the many traditional villages that dot the landscape. The road will also lead you through and into Namibia's many varied wilderness areas, game reserves and national parks, offering vast openness, scores of animals roaming free and great deserts untrappable by man.

A standard vehicle will take you across Namibia's 5,200km of tarred roads, but a four-wheel drive is essential to explore the true depths of Namibia's 35,000km of gravel roads and other unchartered territory. However, even these hardy vehicles can fall prey to the dunes, rocky terrain and sporadic quicksand that await you once you veer off the beaten track. Trying to cut corners or pushing too hard to reach your destination on schedule is your best way to get into the sort of trouble that could dig a hole in your pocket, or worse!

# Map 54 — Lüderitz / Richtersveld National Park

## Grid A1 / B1 — Lüderitz area (Namibia coast)

- **Lüderitz Bucht**
- **Lüderitz** (H, airport, hospital symbols)
- **Dias Cross**
- **Grosse Bucht**
- **Kolmanskop — Ghost Mining Town**
- **Elizabeth Bay**
- **Possession Island**
- Possession Is.
- Albatross Is.
- Pomona Is.
- **Pomona**
- Black Point
- **Bogenfels (Rock Arch)**
- Plumpudding Island
- **Bakers Bay**
- Sinclair's Is.
- Cape Dernburg
- Roastbeef Is.
- Panther Huk
- Salt Flats
- **Elizabeth Bay Ghost Mining Town**
- Tsaukaib
- Haalenberg
- Rotkop
- Grasplatz
- B4
- 58
- NO PUBLIC ACCESS (×3)
- ATLANTIC OCEAN

## Grid A2 / A3 — Richtersveld National Park

Scale: 0 — 10 — 20 km / 0 — 10 miles

- Potjiespram
- Sendelingsdrif
- Kodaspiek ▲ 979 m
- De Koei
- HELSKLOOF GATE
- 924 m ▲
- De Hoop
- Richtersberg
- Kokerboomkloof
- Kuboes
- Vandersterrberg ▲ 1363 m
- Rosyntjieberg ▲ 1329 m
- Mount Terror ▲ 1224 m
- TSWAÏES
- **Wondergat Monument**
- PLOEGBERG ▲ 1214 m
- Cornellsberg ▲ 1374 m
- **Richtersveld National Park**
- NAMIBIA
- SOUTH AFRICA

Distances (km) on tracks: 4.4, 4.3, 10.1, 11.3, 7.3, 5.1, 4.7, 4.6, 4.5, 9.8, 9.1, 11.6, 2.3, 11, 6.7, 9.4, 5.4, 13.2, 11.5, 7.9, 8.2, 15.3, 4.4, 13.8, 18.5, 19.2, 6.3, 8, 8.5

54

# Map: Southern Namibia / Northern South Africa

**Grid references:** C, C13, B4, 59, D, D435, C14

## Namibia

- Garub
- Ausweiche
- Aus
- Klein-Aus Vista
- Ausnek
- Asbospan
- Guibes
- Goageb
- Aukam
- D446
- D459
- D727
- C13
- 1700m
- **HUIB-HOCH PLATEAU**
- Huns
- D463
- **HUNSBERGE**
- Witpütz
- **Proposed Ai-Ais / Richtersveld Transfrontier Park**
- Rosh Pinah
- Konkiep
- Orange (Gariep)
- Sendelingsdrif
- **Richtersveld National Park** (SEE ENLARGED MAP ON PAGE 54)
- Khubus

**KLINGHARD MTS**

**Restricted Area (Former Sperrgebiet)**

NO PUBLIC ACCESS

NO ACCESS

**NAMIBIA**

NO ENTRY

- Oranjemund
- Alexander Bay

## South Africa

- Holgat
- Wreck Point
- Eksteenfontein
- Lekkersing

55

# Map 58: Namib-Naukluft Park and Lüderitz Coast

**A** | **B**

**Row 1:**
- Meob Bay
- Black Reef
- Salt Flats
- Hollandsbird Island
- 62 (to Sossusvlei)
- Sossusvlei
- Sossusvlei and Sand Dunes
- Sesriem Canyon, Sossusvlei Lodge, Sesriem
- Hot-air Balloon Flights
- Kulala Desert Lodge
- Sossusvlei Mountain Lodge

**Row 2:**
- St Francis Bay
- Easter Point
- Easter Cliffs
- Spencer Bay
- Mercury Island
- **Mercury Island Seal Colony**
- Namib-Naukluft Park
- NAMIB DESERT

**Row 3:**
- Simaedjo Point
- ATLANTIC OCEAN
- Hottentot's Bay
- Salt Flats
- Icaboe Island
- Marshall Rocks
- **Icaboe & Neglectus Islands**
- Lüderitz Bucht
- Lüderitz
- Dias Cross
- Grosse Bucht
- Koichab Pan
- B4
- Tsaukaib
- Haalenberg
- Rotkop
- Grasplatz
- Kolmanskop Ghost Mining Town
- 54

58

# Map: Namib-Naukluft Park area

**Grid references:** A, B (columns); 1, 2, 3 (rows)

## Locations and features

- Mile 14
- Rock Bay
- Rössing
- Namib
- Mile 4
- Moon Landscape
- Goanikontes
- Welwitschia Plains
- Tsaobis Leopard Nature Park
- Rock Sculpture Trail
- Wüstenquell Guest Farm
- Tinkas Nature Trail
- Swakopmund
- Welwitschia Drive
- Swakop
- Walvis Bay
- Large, high dunes
- Dune 7
- Namib Desert Park
- Ganab
- Old Rhenish Mission Church
- Walvis Bay Nature Reserve
- Rooibank
- Sandwich Harbour
- Namib-Naukluft Park
- Zebra Pan
- Gobabeb Desert Research Centre (No Entry)
- Homeb
- Kuiseb
- Black Cliff
- Conception Bay
- Tsondab Vlei
- NAMIB DESERT
- Salt Flats
- Meob Bay
- Black Reef
- Sesriem Canyon
- Hot-air Balloon Flights
- Sossusvlei
- Hollandsbird Island
- Sossusvlei and Sand Dunes

## Roads
- B2
- C14
- C28
- C34
- D1914
- D1985

## Distances (km)
31, 67, 114, 34, 40, 58, 52, 22, 54, 24, 12, 54, 28, 53, 11, 53, 16, 33, 17, 24, 8, 58

62

# Map of Namibia — Windhoek and Namib-Naukluft Region

**Regions and Areas:**
- KHOMAS HOCHLAND
- Khomas
- NAMIBIA
- HAKOSBERGE
- NAUKLUFT
- TSARISBERGE

**Towns and Places:**
- Windhoek
- Eros
- Fort
- Haris
- Aris
- Bergland
- Wortel
- Us
- Chaibis
- Naos
- Rehoboth
- Reho Spa Recreation Resort
- Nauchas
- Klein Aub
- Nauzerus
- Rietoog
- Schlip
- Solitaire
- Büllsport
- Haruchas
- Nomtsas
- Neuras
- Maltahöhe
- Sesriem

**Passes:**
- Bosua Pass
- Kuiseb Pass
- Gaub Pass
- Gamsberg Pass
- Spreetshoogte Pass
- Remhoogte Pass

**Points of Interest:**
- Daan Viljoen Game Park
- Von François Fort (68)
- Historic German Building
- Kupferberg
- Weissenfels Guest Farm
- Hakos Guest Farm
- Lake Oanob Resort
- Kuiseb Canyon
- Rostock Ritz
- Namibgrens Rest Camp
- Dassie Trails
- Spectacular view of Namib
- Camel Safaris
- Solitaire Country Lodge
- Ababis Guest Farm 1973m
- Namib-Naukluft Lodge
- Weltevrede Rest Camp
- Namib Rest Camp
- Naukluft 4x4 Trail
- Olive Trail
- Büllsport Guest Farm
- Waterkloof Trail
- Nauklauft Hiking Trail
- Sossusvlei Lodge
- Tsauchab River Camping
- Zebra River Lodge
- Betesda Guest Farm
- Kulala Desert Lodge
- Sossusvlei Wilderness Camp
- Sossusvlei Mountain Lodge
- Namseb Game Lodge
- 1895m

**Rivers:**
- Usib
- Tsondab
- Tsauchab
- Fish

**Roads:**
- B1, B6
- C14, C19, C21, C24, C26, C27, C28
- MR47
- D845, D850, D854, D855, D860, D861, D831, D1206, D1237, D1254, D1259, D1261, D1262, D1265, D1282, D1283, D1290, D1414, D1953, D1958, D1976, D1980, D1982

**Grid References:** C, D, 59, 63, 64, 68

# Map: Kaokoland / Skeleton Coast / Kunene

**A** | **B**

## Kaokoland

**1**

- Okandjombo (D3707, 45)
- Oruwanje
- Kaoko Otavi (D3705) — **79**
- JOUBERTBERGE (C43)
- Otjitoko (D3709, 60)
- Robbie's Pass (51)
- Okatumba (19, 22)
- Otjikondavirongo
- Otjondeka (D3708, 35)
- Ombombo
- Otjitunduwa (12)
- **Dorslandtrekkers Monument**
- Purros (34) — D3707
- Tomakas (30)
- Ganamub (30) / Ganamub river
- Otjitaimo (D3705, 49)
- Otjomatemba (C43, 32) — D3710, 96
- Sesfontein (11)
- **Old Fort** / Fort Sesfontein (H)
- **Blinkwater Falls**
- Warmquelle (22)
- Hoanib (71)
- Dubis
- Khowarib (D3706)
- Baadjie (23)
- Khowarib
- Ombonde (60)

**2**

- NO ENTRY
- Amspoort
- **Kunene**
- NO PUBLIC ACCESS
- Skeleton Coast Park
- Etendeka Mountain Camp
- Palmwag Lodge
- Palmwag (C43, 82)
- Grootberg Pass (C40, 41)
- Terrace Bay
- Dune Point
- Shallow Breakers — C34 (31)
- Uniab

**3**

- Torra Bay (18, 10)
- Salt Flats
- Palgrave Pt
- Wereldsend (58)
- Bergsig (C43, 44)
- **SPRINGBOK WASSER GATE** (C39, 33)
- Koichab
- Damaraland Wilderness Camp (40)
- Huab
- Twyfelfontein Country Lodge
- **Twyfelfontein Rock Engraving**
- **66**

72

# Etosha National Park

**Natukanaoka Pan**

Cuvelai and Etosha Pan

**NEHALE LYA MPINGANA GATE**
Andoni
**Toilet**

**VON LINDEQUIST GATE**

Etosha Pan

Groot Okevi
Historic Fort
Okerfontein
Klein Okevi
Namutoni
**Toilet**
C38

Springbokfontein
**Toilet**
Chudob

Okondeka
Rietfontein
Halali
Kalkheuwel
**Toilet**
**Toilet**

**Toilet**
**Moringa Forest**
Okaukuejo
Okaukuejo
Aus
**ANDERSSON GATE**

Ongava Lodge

C38
Toshari Inn

D2695
D2779
D2782
D2782
D2865
D2866

D2710
C39
D2873

D2780
D2782
D2761
D2775
D2869
D2468
D2869

D2696
Neina
**Gamkarab Cave**

Goreis
C40
Nugubaes
Outjo
D2773
Okaputa
Otjikango
D2433

C39
Vrindskap
Hartseer
Okave
Otjenga
Heuningberg

Ugab
C38
D2430
D2505

D2752
Otjitasu
**Otjiwarongo**
Otjibamba Lodge

D2417
C33
B1
C22
Erundu
Ozondjache

# A    B

**1**

Serra Cafema Lodge
Cunene
Otjinungwa
17°14'50"S 12°25'09"E GPS

OTJIHIPA MTS

HARTMANN MTS

17°28'04"S 13°03'41"E GPS
Etengwa

17°33'18"S 12°33'14"E GPS

17°37'25"S 12°51'29"E GPS
Okauwe
D3703

Van Zyl's Pass
Otjitanda

17°47'49"S 12°31'22"E GPS

17°39'20"S 12°41'43"E GPS

17°46'56"S 12°57'43"E GPS

Salt Flats

NO ENTRY

17°47'23"S 12°23'20"E GPS

NO ENTRY

**2**

Salt Flats

NO ENTRY

Orupembe

18°04'18"S 12°44'29"E GPS

18°09'22"S 12°33'38"E GPS

Sanitatas
Okandjombo

Cape Fria

ETENDEKA

NO ENTRY

Skeleton Coast Park

Public Access Restricted

Skeleton Coast Camp
NO ENTRY
Purros

**3**

Rocky Point
Hoarusib

ATLANTIC OCEAN

78

# C

**Epupa Falls** / **Dramatic Waterfall**

Epupa Falls GPS
17°00'09"S
13°14'39"E

**C43**

Enyandi

**ZEBRA MTS**

17°13'40"S
13°14'11"E
GPS

Omuhonga

D3700

17°26'01"S
13°16'20"E
GPS

Okangwati

Ondoto

Swartbooisdrift

17°20'28"S
13°50'56"E
GPS

**Ruacana Falls**

Epembe

Otjiveze

D3702

Kunene River Lodge

Ehomba

**Otjijandjasemo Hot Spring**

**STEILRAND MTS**

D3700

17°51'45"S
13°01'26"E
GPS

Etanga

Otjivero

D3703

18°03'29"S
13°15'31"E
GPS

**Opuwo**

**GIRAFFEN MTS**

Hoarusib

Otjiu

**Spring**

D3707

**Dorsland Trek Church Ruin**

Oruwanje

D3705

Kaoko Otavi

**C43**

D3710

**JOUBERTBERGE**

Okatumba

**Kaokoland**

*Robbie's Pass*

Otjikondavirongo

D3705

D3708

Ombombo

Otjitunduwa

**Dorslandtrekkers Monument**

D3707

Otjitaimo

Otjomatemba

D3710

Tomakas

Ganamub

**C43**

Ganamub

Sesfontein

**Blinkwater Falls**

Kowares

**Old Fort**

Fort Sesfontein

**C43**

Warmquelle

D3706

Hoanib

Dubis

Khowarib

Khowarib

Baadjie

Aasvoëlbad

**KUNENE**

# D

**ANGOLA**

**View of Waterfall**

17°24'46"S
14°21'19"E
GPS

Ruacana

D361

**State Forest**

**C35**

18°08'39"S
14°17'26"E
GPS

**C41**

D3709

Otjitoko

**C35**

Otjondeka

Okatjiur

**C35**

# A B

**Calueque**
Ombala-io-Mungo
**Naulila**

1

7°24'46"S
4°21'19"E

Ruacana — Mahenene — **Uutapi (Ombalantu)** — D3608 — Okalongo — D3608 — Ongenga
C46
43
40
35
Onesi
D3611 32
D3609
38
20
45 D3616 36 D3612
Ogongo
Oshikuku
Okatana
10
26
Tsandi
D3612
Oshakati
25 C41 D3619
Ongwediva
**Okahao**
26
Onaanda
Etilyasa

**Oshana**

2

**Omusati**

**NAMIBIA**

D3605

State Forest

Western area of park open to
registered tour operators only

N atukanaoka
Pan

3

Duineveld   N omab   Tobieroen   Sonderkop   Ozonjuitji m'Bari
48        21       22                47
owares  Dolomietpunt       Teespoed    Duiwelsvuur
9                                          **Toilet**
Bateldraf        Okawao                              24
Aasvoelbad   Jakkalswater          Charl Marais      22
                                   Pan         **Moringa Forest**
31
Otjovasandu   D2763   D2697   D2697  26  73

80

# A  B

## ANGOLA

**1**

State Forest

Okongo ✈ 🅿
D3405 56
110 C45 D3404 35 D3407
45 Ekoko Mpungu 28
22 Nepara

**2** Oshikoto

Tsitsib

## NAMIBIA

25
Oshivelo
*Ovambo* 10
tosha Aoba Lodge D3001
8 19 D3004 22
6 D3028 Tsintsabis ✈
VON LINDEQUIST GATE 18 5 18 22 Giant Baobab Tree
14 21 D3016
Mokuti Lodge D3003 B1 23 D3007 D3047 34 C83 27 D2855 28
**3** 26 54 42 D3017 29 35
37 tosha National Park 14 D3039 D2848
Lake D3025 D3043 Lake 16 17 16 9 17 Roy's Rest Camp
Guinas 19 Otjikoto C83
D3028 Guinas Bobos H ⛺ Tsumeb D3021 D2858 17 42
82 D2866 25 75 B1 6 ✈ 🅿 🚉 ⛽ ✚ ⛽ 33 Abenab B8

## A | B

**1**
- Mutango
- Utokota
- B8 50 Mashari 20
- Cuito
- Mucusso National Park
- Dirico
- Nyangana
- D3400
- Taratara
- 56
- B8 81
- D3309
- D3403
- 101
- 83

**Kavango**

**2**
- Tamsu
- Khaudum
- Nxamasere
- Doringstraat Waterhole
- Khaudum Game Park
- Elands Drink Waterhole
- Dussi Waterhole
- Samagaigai
- Sikereti
- Nhoma
- Soncana Waterhole

**3**
- Nhoma
- N homa
- D3312
- D3303
- D3311
- Aasvoëlnes
- Klein Dobe
- D3303
- **Dorsland Trek Baobab**
- C44 27
- D3301
- 29
- 14
- Tsumkwe Lodge
- Tsumkwe
- Holboam
- Makuri
- DOBE
- Quankwa
- 26
- 31
- 35
- **Otjozondjupa**
- **Holboom**
- Djokwe
- **Grootboom (Giant Baobab Tree)**
- D3302
- D3303
- Tweeputte
- 42
- 77
- Caecae (Xaixai)
- 9

84

# C D

## ANGOLA

Caprivi Strip

Mucusso

Caprivi Game Park

B8 200

Mukwe

Divundu

Popa Falls

Suclabo Lodge

Omega

Bwabwata National Park
*Proposed alteration to Caprivi Game Park*

Ndhovu Safari Lodge

Mahango Game Park

86

**MOHEMBO**

Drotsky's Cabins

Shakawe

Shakawe Fishing Lodge

Sengoshe

Okavango

Tsodilo Hills

R

Nxamasere

Dibebe

Mawana

Dungu

**Rock Paintings**

Sepupa

Swamp Stop

Cada

Gqoro

Seronga

Eretse

Guma Lagoon

Etshao

Xaudum

Makwena Lodge

Jedibe

Ngogo

Etsha 6

Qhaakwe

Momba
Momba Island
Xigera

Thaoge

Abu's

Gumare

Okavango Delta

SANDVELDT TONGUE

Xudum

Macatee

Nokaneng

Thaoge

88

85

# A
# B

**85**

Cada  Seronga  Eretse
Gqoro
Guma Lagoon
Etsha
Makwena Lodge
Jedibe
Etsha 6
Qhaakwe
*Xaudum*
Abu's
Gumare
*Thaoge*
Okavango Delta

**1**

**77**

Nokaneng

SANDVELD

**2**  Gcwihaba (Drotsky's) Cave

*Thaoge*

Tsau

**71**

Sehithwa

**3**

88

# Index

| NAME | GRID | PG | NAME | GRID | PG | NAME | GRID | PG |
|---|---|---|---|---|---|---|---|---|
| Aasvoëlnes | A3 | 84 | Divundu | C1 | 85 | Goageb | D3 | 59 |
| Aasvoëlnes | C2 | 77 | Djokwe | A3 | 84 | Gobabeb | B2 | 62 |
| Abenab | B3 | 82 | Djokwe | C2 | 77 | Gobabis | A3 | 70 |
| Abenab | D2 | 75 | Dordabis | A1 | 64 | Gochas | C1 | 61 |
| Ai-Ais | A2 | 56 | Doreenville | B1 | 64 | Gochas | C3 | 65 |
| Akanous | D1 | 61 | Doreenville | D3 | 69 | Goodhouse | B3 | 56 |
| Akanous | D1 | 65 | Doros | C1 | 67 | Goreis | A3 | 74 |
| Alexander Bay | C3 | 55 | Drimiopsis | A3 | 70 | Gqoro | B1 | 88 |
| Ameib | D2 | 67 | Du Plessis | B2 | 70 | Gqoro | D2 | 85 |
| Aminuis | D1 | 65 | Dubis | A2 | 72 | Grootberg | C2 | 73 |
| Amspoort | A2 | 72 | Dubis | C3 | 79 | Grootfontein | D1 | 59 |
| Andoni | B1 | 74 | Duineveld | A2 | 64 | Grootfontein | D2 | 75 |
| Andoni | D3 | 81 | Dungu | D2 | 85 | Gross Ums | C1 | 65 |
| Arandis | D3 | 67 | Eenhana | C1 | 81 | Grünau | B2 | 56 |
| Aranos | C3 | 65 | Ehomba | D1 | 79 | Guinas | A3 | 82 |
| Ariamsvlei | D2 | 57 | Eindpaal | C2 | 61 | Guinas | C2 | 75 |
| Aris | B3 | 68 | Eirup | B3 | 64 | Gumare | B1 | 88 |
| Aris | D1 | 63 | Ekoko | A2 | 82 | Gumare | D3 | 85 |
| Aroab | D1 | 57 | Eksteenfontein | A3 | 56 | Gunab | A3 | 60 |
| Aroab | D3 | 61 | Eksteenfontein | D3 | 55 | Gweta | B2 | 90 |
| Asab | B2 | 60 | Elundu | D1 | 81 | Hanaus | A2 | 60 |
| Aukam | D1 | 55 | Engela | C1 | 81 | Haribes | A1 | 60 |
| Aus | C1 | 55 | Enyandi | C1 | 79 | Haribes | A3 | 64 |
| Aus | C3 | 59 | Epembe | C1 | 79 | Haris | B3 | 68 |
| Aussenkehr | A3 | 56 | Epembe | C2 | 81 | Haris | D1 | 63 |
| Baadjie | B2 | 72 | Epukiro | B2 | 70 | Hartseer | B3 | 74 |
| Baadjie | D3 | 79 | Epupa | D1 | 67 | Haruchas | C3 | 63 |
| Bergsig | B3 | 72 | Epupa | D3 | 73 | Hebron | C1 | 69 |
| Berseba | A2 | 60 | Eremutua | A1 | 68 | Helena | C2 | 71 |
| Bethanie | A3 | 60 | Eretse | B1 | 88 | Helmeringhausen | D2 | 59 |
| Bethanie | D3 | 59 | Eretse | D2 | 85 | Henties Bay | C3 | 67 |
| Betsaa | A2 | 86 | Erundu | B1 | 68 | Heuningberg | B3 | 74 |
| Biermanskool | D2 | 73 | Erundu | B3 | 74 | Hoaseb | C1 | 65 |
| Bladgrond | D3 | 57 | Esere | C3 | 75 | Hochveld | C2 | 69 |
| Brack | A1 | 64 | Etanga | C2 | 79 | Hohental | C2 | 75 |
| Brack | C3 | 69 | Etemba | A2 | 68 | Homeb | B2 | 62 |
| Brandberg West | B1 | 66 | Etemba | D2 | 67 | Hottentot's Bay | A3 | 58 |
| Brukkaros | B2 | 60 | Etengwa | B1 | 78 | Huams | D2 | 59 |
| Buitepos | C3 | 71 | Etilyasa | B2 | 80 | Huns | A1 | 56 |
| Bukalo | C1 | 87 | Etjo | B1 | 68 | Huns | D1 | 55 |
| Bulwana | B1 | 60 | Etsha 6 | B1 | 88 | Inachab | A1 | 56 |
| Bushman Pits | A2 | 90 | Etsha 6 | D3 | 85 | Kachekabwe | C1 | 87 |
| Cada | B1 | 88 | Etsha | B1 | 88 | Kakus | A3 | 70 |
| Cada | D2 | 85 | Etsha | D2 | 85 | Kakus | C1 | 65 |
| Caecae (Xaixai) | B3 | 84 | Evero | B2 | 68 | Kalkrand | A2 | 64 |
| Caecae (Xaixai) | D2 | 77 | Fransfontein | D3 | 73 | Kalkveld | A1 | 68 |
| Calai | D2 | 83 | Gagarus | D2 | 73 | Kamanjab | C2 | 73 |
| Calueque | A1 | 80 | Gainatseb | D3 | 73 | Kano Vlei | B2 | 76 |
| Cauas | D3 | 73 | Gam | D3 | 77 | Kano Vlei | D3 | 83 |
| Chaibis | C1 | 63 | Ganab | B1 | 62 | Kanyu | A2 | 90 |
| Coblenz | D3 | 75 | Ganamub | A1 | 72 | Kaoko Otavi | B1 | 72 |
| Cuangar | C1 | 83 | Ganamub | C3 | 79 | Kaoko Otavi | C2 | 79 |
| Dabenoris | B3 | 56 | Garib | A1 | 64 | Kapp's Farm | A1 | 64 |
| Derm | B2 | 64 | Garinais | C3 | 61 | Kapp's Farm | C3 | 69 |
| Dibebe | D2 | 85 | Gibeon | A1 | 60 | Karakuwisa | B1 | 76 |
| Dirico | B1 | 84 | Girib | A2 | 64 | Karakuwisa | D3 | 83 |
| Dis Al | A2 | 70 | Goageb | D1 | 55 | Karasburg | B2 | 56 |

91

# Index

| NAME | GRID | PG | NAME | GRID | PG | NAME | GRID | PG |
|---|---|---|---|---|---|---|---|---|
| Karibib | A2 | 68 | Mooifontein | D2 | 59 | Okandjombo | B2 | 78 |
| Kasane | D1 | 87 | Mopipi | A3 | 90 | Okangwati | C1 | 79 |
| Kataba | C1 | 87 | Moremaoto | A2 | 90 | Okankolo | C2 | 81 |
| Katima Mulilo | C1 | 87 | Motopi | A2 | 90 | Okarukurume | A2 | 70 |
| Kavimba | C1 | 87 | Motsomi | D1 | 65 | Okarukurume | D2 | 69 |
| Kazungula | D1 | 87 | Mpungu | B2 | 82 | Okasewa | B1 | 64 |
| Keetmanshoop | B3 | 60 | Muchenje | C1 | 87 | Okasewa | D3 | 69 |
| Keitsas | A3 | 70 | Mucusso | C1 | 85 | Okatana | B1 | 80 |
| Keitsas | C1 | 65 | Mukwe | C1 | 85 | Okatjiura | B1 | 72 |
| Khaudum | B2 | 84 | Mururani | A1 | 76 | Okatjiura | D3 | 79 |
| Khaudum | D1 | 77 | Mururani | C3 | 83 | Okatumba | B1 | 72 |
| Khorixas | C3 | 73 | Mutango | A1 | 84 | Okatumba | C3 | 79 |
| Khowarib | B2 | 72 | Mutango | D2 | 83 | Okatuwo | B2 | 70 |
| Khowarib | D3 | 79 | Nabies | D3 | 57 | Okaukuejo | A1 | 74 |
| Khubus | D3 | 55 | Nama Pan | D3 | 77 | Okaukuejo | C3 | 81 |
| Khumaga | A3 | 90 | Namutoni | B1 | 74 | Okauwe | B1 | 78 |
| Klein Aub | D2 | 63 | Namutoni | D3 | 81 | Okavarumendu | A2 | 70 |
| Klein Dobe | A3 | 84 | Nanzes | B2 | 56 | Okave | B3 | 74 |
| Klein Dobe | C2 | 77 | Naos | D1 | 63 | Okombahe | D2 | 67 |
| Klein Nauas | B2 | 64 | Narubis | B1 | 56 | Okondjatu | D1 | 69 |
| Klein-Karas | B2 | 56 | Nauchas | C2 | 63 | Okongo | A1 | 82 |
| Koës | C2 | 61 | Naulila | A1 | 80 | Okovimburu | B2 | 70 |
| Kokerboom | C2 | 57 | Nauzerus | C2 | 63 | Okozondara | A2 | 70 |
| Kolmanskop | B1 | 54 | Ncaute | C1 | 77 | Olukonda | C2 | 81 |
| Kolmanskop | B3 | 58 | Ncaute | D2 | 83 | Omahoro | D1 | 67 |
| Komukanti | C2 | 75 | Neina | B3 | 74 | Omaruru | A2 | 68 |
| Kongola | A1 | 86 | Neineis | D2 | 67 | Omatako | B2 | 68 |
| Kowares | A3 | 80 | Neisip | D3 | 59 | Omatjete | D1 | 67 |
| Kowares | C1 | 73 | Nepara | B2 | 82 | Ombala-io-Mungo | A1 | 80 |
| Kowares | D3 | 79 | Neuras | C1 | 59 | Ombombo | B1 | 72 |
| Lekkersing | D3 | 55 | Neuras | C3 | 63 | Ombombo | D3 | 79 |
| Leonardville | C2 | 65 | Ngoma | C1 | 87 | Omega | D1 | 85 |
| Lidfontein | B3 | 64 | Nhoma | A3 | 84 | Omitara | D3 | 69 |
| Linyandi | B1 | 86 | Nhoma | B2 | 84 | Omulunga | C2 | 81 |
| Lüderitz | B1 | 54 | Nhoma. | C2 | 77 | Omundaungilo | D1 | 81 |
| Lüderitz | B3 | 58 | Nhoma | D1 | 77 | Onaanda | B2 | 80 |
| Luhebu | B2 | 76 | Nina | B1 | 64 | Ondangwa | C2 | 81 |
| Luiana | A1 | 86 | Nkurenkuru | C1 | 83 | Onderombapa | D1 | 65 |
| Maanlig | A2 | 76 | Noenieput | D2 | 57 | Ondjiva | C1 | 81 |
| Maanlig | C3 | 83 | Nokaneng | B2 | 88 | Ondobe | C1 | 81 |
| Mabale | C1 | 87 | Nokaneng | D3 | 85 | Onesi | A1 | 80 |
| Mahenene | A1 | 80 | Nomtsas | D3 | 63 | Ongenga | B1 | 80 |
| Maiuvo | C2 | 83 | Noordoewer | A3 | 56 | Ongwediva | B2 | 80 |
| Makalamabedi | D2 | 89 | Nugubaes | A3 | 74 | Oniipa | C2 | 81 |
| Maltahöhe | D1 | 59 | Nxamasere | C2 | 85 | Onseepkans | C3 | 57 |
| Maltahöhe | D3 | 63 | Nyangana | B1 | 84 | Onyati | C2 | 81 |
| Mangetti | A1 | 76 | Obobogorab | D1 | 57 | Opuwo | D2 | 77 |
| Mangetti | C3 | 83 | Ogongo | B1 | 80 | Oranjemund | C3 | 55 |
| Mariental | B1 | 60 | Ohangwena | C1 | 81 | Orupembe | B2 | 78 |
| Mariental | B3 | 64 | Okahandja | B2 | 68 | Orusewa | D1 | 67 |
| Maroelaboom | A2 | 76 | Okahao | A2 | 80 | Orusewa | D3 | 73 |
| Maroelaboom | C3 | 83 | Okakarara | C1 | 69 | Oruwanje | A1 | 72 |
| Mashari | A1 | 84 | Okakarara | C3 | 75 | Oruwanje | C2 | 79 |
| Maun | C2 | 89 | Okalongo | B1 | 80 | Osamba | D3 | 69 |
| Mawana | D2 | 85 | Okamatapati | D1 | 69 | Oshakati | B2 | 80 |
| Mmatshumo | A3 | 90 | Okamatapati | D3 | 75 | Oshigambo | C2 | 81 |
| Mon Desir | D2 | 73 | Okandjombo | A1 | 72 | Oshikango | C1 | 81 |

# Index

| NAME | GRID | PG | NAME | GRID | PG | NAME | GRID | PG |
|---|---|---|---|---|---|---|---|---|
| Oshikuku | B1 | 80 | Quankwa | D2 | 77 | Tomakas | C3 | 79 |
| Oshititu | D2 | 81 | Rakops | A3 | 90 | Tondoro | C2 | 83 |
| Oshivelo | A3 | 82 | Rehoboth | D2 | 63 | Torra Bay | A3 | 72 |
| Oshivelo | C1 | 75 | Rietfontein | D1 | 57 | Toteng | C2 | 89 |
| Oshivelo | D3 | 81 | Rietfontein | D2 | 71 | Tsandi | A2 | 80 |
| Osire | C1 | 69 | Rietfontein | D2 | 75 | Tsaraxaibis | C2 | 57 |
| Otavi | C2 | 75 | Rietfontein | D3 | 61 | Tsau | B2 | 88 |
| Otjahevita | C3 | 75 | Rietoog | D2 | 63 | Tses | B2 | 60 |
| Otjenga | B3 | 74 | Rooibank | A1 | 62 | Tsintsabis | B3 | 82 |
| Otjihorongo | D1 | 67 | Rosh Pinah | D2 | 55 | Tsintsabis | D1 | 75 |
| Otjikango | B3 | 74 | Ruacana | A1 | 80 | Tsitsib | B2 | 82 |
| Otjikondavirongo | A2 | 71 | Ruacana | D1 | 79 | Tsoe | A3 | 90 |
| Otjikondavirongo | C3 | 79 | Rundu | D2 | 83 | Tsootsha | D3 | 71 |
| Otjiveze | C1 | 79 | Rupara | C2 | 83 | Tsumeb | A3 | 82 |
| Otjikondo | D2 | 73 | Samagaigai | A3 | 84 | Tsumeb | C2 | 75 |
| Otjimbingwe | A3 | 68 | Samagaigai | C2 | 77 | Tsumkwe | A3 | 84 |
| Otjimbovo | A2 | 68 | Sambusu | D2 | 83 | Tsumkwe | C2 | 77 |
| Otjimukandi | A3 | 70 | Sangwali | B2 | 86 | Tubusis | D2 | 67 |
| Otjinene | A1 | 70 | Sanitatas | B2 | 78 | Tutara | D3 | 73 |
| Otjinoko | B2 | 70 | Satau | C1 | 87 | Twee Rivier | C2 | 61 |
| Otjinungwa | B1 | 78 | Savuti | B2 | 86 | Tweeputte | C3 | 77 |
| Otjisemba | B2 | 68 | Schlip | A2 | 64 | Uhlenhorst | B2 | 64 |
| Otjitambi | D2 | 73 | Schlip | D2 | 63 | Uis | C2 | 67 |
| Otjitanda | B1 | 78 | Seeheim | A1 | 56 | Union's End | D1 | 61 |
| Otjitasu | A1 | 68 | Seeheim | A3 | 60 | Union's End | D1 | 65 |
| Otjitasu | A3 | 74 | Sehithwa | B2 | 88 | Usakos | D2 | 67 |
| Otjitoko | B1 | 72 | Sendelingsdrif | D2 | 55 | Us | C1 | 63 |
| Otjitoko | D2 | 79 | Sengoshe | D2 | 85 | Utokota | A1 | 84 |
| Otjitunduwa | B1 | 72 | Sepupa | D2 | 85 | Uutapi(Ombalantu) | A1 | 80 |
| Otjituuo | A2 | 76 | Seronga | B1 | 88 | Velloorsdrif | C3 | 57 |
| Otjiu | C2 | 79 | Seronga | D2 | 85 | Vioolsdrif | A3 | 56 |
| Otjiwarongo | B1 | 68 | Sesfontein | B2 | 72 | Vogelweide | C2 | 65 |
| Otjiwarongo | B3 | 74 | Sesfontein | C3 | 79 | Vredeshoop | C1 | 57 |
| Otjiyarwa | B2 | 70 | Shakawe | C2 | 85 | Vrindskap | A3 | 74 |
| Otjomatemba | B1 | 72 | Shorobe | B3 | 86 | Walvis Bay | A1 | 62 |
| Otjomatemba | D3 | 79 | Shorobe | D2 | 89 | Warmbad | B3 | 56 |
| Otjondeka | B1 | 72 | Sibinda | B1 | 86 | Warmfontein | C1 | 57 |
| Otjondeka | D3 | 79 | Sikereti | B3 | 84 | Warmquelle | B2 | 72 |
| Otjosondu | D2 | 69 | Sikereti | D2 | 77 | Warmquelle | D3 | 79 |
| Otjovasandu | A3 | 80 | Solitaire | C2 | 63 | Wegdraai | C2 | 61 |
| Otjovasandu | C2 | 73 | Sorris Sorris | C1 | 67 | Weissbrünn | C2 | 73 |
| Otjumue | A2 | 68 | Stampriet | B3 | 64 | Welverdiend | D2 | 61 |
| Otjumue | D2 | 67 | Steinhausen | D2 | 69 | Wereldsend | B3 | 72 |
| Outjo | A3 | 74 | Sukses | B1 | 68 | Wilhelmstal | A2 | 68 |
| Ozondati | D1 | 67 | Sukwane | A3 | 90 | Windhoek | B3 | 68 |
| Ozondjache | B1 | 68 | Summerdown | A2 | 70 | Windhoek | D1 | 63 |
| Ozondjache | B3 | 74 | Summerdown | D2 | 69 | Witbooisvlei | B1 | 60 |
| Palmwag | B3 | 72 | Swakopmund | A1 | 62 | Witpütz | D2 | 55 |
| Pandamatenga | D2 | 87 | Swakopmund | C3 | 67 | Witvlei | A3 | 70 |
| Parakarungu | C1 | 87 | Swartbooisdrift | D1 | 79 | Wlotzkas Baken | C3 | 67 |
| Pella | C3 | 57 | Talismanis | D2 | 71 | Xanagas | C3 | 71 |
| Persip | C2 | 61 | Tamsu | A2 | 84 | Xhumo | A3 | 90 |
| Phuduhudu | A2 | 90 | Tamsu | D1 | 77 | Zaris | C1 | 59 |
| Pomona | B1 | 54 | Taratara | A1 | 84 | | | |
| Purros | A1 | 72 | Terrace Bay | A3 | 72 | | | |
| Purros | B3 | 78 | Tjirundo | A2 | 68 | | | |
| Quankwa | B3 | 84 | Tomakas | A1 | 72 | | | |

# Resources

## NAMIBIAN CONTACT DETAILS & INFORMATION

Namibia (country code 09264)

**Namibian tourism board**
Tel: (061) 290 6000
Fax: (061) 254 848

**Tourist Information**
Tel: (061) 285 7000
Fax: (061) 248567

**Namibia Wildlife Resorts**
Tel: (061) 236975

**Police**
The national emergency number for the Police is 10111.

**Telephone enquiries**
For numbers that have changed or are not listed in the telephone directory, dial 1188.

**Gobabis (062)**
Tourist office
Tel: 562 428
Fax: 562 359

Omaheke Tourist info centre
Tel: 562 270
Fax: 562 551

Municipality
Tel: 56 2566
Fax: 56 3012

**Grootfontein (067)**
Tourist office
Tel: 242 548
Fax: 242 128

Tourist info
Tel: 243100

Municipality
Tel: 24 3101
Fax: 24 2930

**Henties Bay (064)**
Tourist office
Tel: 501143
Fax: 501143

Namib info
Tel: 500 880

Municipality
Tel: 50 0007
Fax: 50 0521

**Katima Mulilo (066)**
Tourist office
Tel: 25 3027
Fax: 25 3322

Tutwa tourism and travel
Tel: 253 048

Municipality
Tel: 253586
Fax: 25 3212

**Keetmanshoop (063)**
Tourist office
Tel: 223 223
Fax: 223 955

Southern Tourist Forum
Tel: 221 266
Fax: 223 813

Municipality
Tel: 22 1212
Fax: 22 3818

**Lüderitz (063)**
Tourist office
Tel: 202811
Fax: 204188

Municipality
Tel: 20 2041
Fax: 20 2971

**Mariental (063)**
Tourist office
Tel: 242 427
Fax: 242 366

Municipality
Tel: 24 0347
Fax: 24 2039

**Okahandja (062)**
Tourist office
Tel: 501 091
Fax: 501 805

Municipality
Tel: 50 1051
Fax: 50 1746

**Omaruru (064)**
Tourist office
Tel: 571 194
Fax: 570 105

Municipality
Tel: 57 0104
Fax: 57 0105

**Opuwo (065)**
Tourist office
Tel: 273003
Fax: 273171

The Kaoko Info Centre
Tel: 273420
Fax: 273003

Municipality
Tel: 27 3007
Fax: 27 3032

**Oshakati (065)**
Tourist office
Tel: 220805
Fax: 222824

Municipality
Tel: 22 0805
Fax: 22 0435

**Otavi (067)**
Tourist office
Tel: 234022
Fax: 234236

Municipality
Tel: 23 4152
Fax: 23 4236

**Otjiwarongo (067)**
Tourist office
Tel: 302 645
Fax: 303309

Municipality
Tel: 30 2231
Fax: 30 2098

**Outjo (067)**
Tourist Office
Tel: 313436
Fax: 313593

Informal Etosha
Tel: 313072

Municipality
Tel: 31 3013
Fax: 31 3065

**Rehoboth (062)**
Tourist office
Tel: 523 202
Fax: 524 257

Municipality
Tel: 52 2090
Fax: 52 2091

# Resources

## TOURIST INFORMATION

**Rundu (066)**
Tourist office
Tel: 255 749
Fax: 255 431

Municipality
Tel: 25 5040
Fax: 25 6718

**Sesfontein (065)**
Fort Sesfontein lodge
Tel: 275 534

**Swakopmund (064)**
Tourist office
Tel: 410 4332
Fax: 403 236

Municipality
Tel: 410 4327
Fax: 410 4213

**Tsumeb (067)**
Tourist office
Tel: 229084
Fax: 229091

Travel North Namibia
Tel: 220 728

Municipality
Tel: 22 1056
Fax: 22 1464

**Walvis Bay (064)**
Tourist office
Tel: 201 3267
Fax: 205 971

Walvis Bay Information
Tel: 209 170
Fax: 209 171

Tourist info centre
Tel: 205 981
Fax: 204 528

Municipality
Tel: 201 3111
Fax: 20 4528

**Windhoek (061)**
Tourist office
Tel: 290 2058
Fax: 290 2092

Municipality
Tel: 29 02911
Fax: 29 02064

### Entry Requirements
All visitors must have a valid passport, and temporary residence permits for visitors are issued on arrival and allow tourists a period of 90 days in the country. Bona fide tourists and business travellers from many countries are exempted from visa requirements (enquire with your travel agent). Visitors are, however, advised to confirm visa requirements with their travel agent.

### Health Requirements
Vaccinations against smallpox, cholera and yellow fever are not required. However, visitors travelling from or through countries where yellow fever is endemic must have a valid International Certificate of Vaccination. This requirement does not apply to air travellers in transit. No AIDS screening tests are conducted.

### Air Travel
Hosea Kutako International Airport, 45km (28 miles) west of the capital, is the major point of entry into Namibia. Eros Airport, 4km (2.5 miles) from the city centre, is served by domestic flights. Air Namibia, the national carrier, has regular scheduled flights to Katima Mulilo, Lüderitz, Ondangwa, Oranjemund, Swakopmund and Walvis Bay. There are landing strips throughout the country and air-charter services are available in Windhoek, Swakopmund and Walvis Bay.

### Road Travel
Namibia has a well-developed road system, covering some 40,000km (24,856 miles). Trunk roads covering 5000km (3107 miles) are tarred and connect all the main centres, while major gravel-surface roads are generally in a good condition. The state of district and farm roads varies from good to poor, depending on when they were last graded.

MOTORING TIPS: During the summer months care should be exercised on gravel-surface roads as washaways are common after rains. Motorists should look out for wild or domestic animals as they can cause serious accidents. Warthogs feed in the long grass alongside the road and are in the habit of suddenly crossing it. Kudu are a danger at night in densely vegetated areas, and warning signs should be heeded. In rural areas, domestic animals are not fenced so be careful. Always carry emergency spares and sufficient water (at least 10 litres; 2.6 gallons), especially on the lonely backroads. Driver's licence: The carrying of driver's licences is now compulsory. Foreign licences are acceptable if they carry a photograph and are either printed in English or accompanied by an English-language certificate of authenticity. An alternative is to obtain an International Driving Permit before departing for Namibia. Licences issued in Botswana, Lesotho, South Africa, Swaziland and Zimbabwe are valid.

ROAD RULES AND SIGNS: In Namibia one drives on the left-hand side of the road. The speed limit on major roads is 120kph (75mph) and in urban areas 60kph (37mph), unless otherwise indicated. Depending on the condition of gravel-surface roads, the recommended speed is between 80kph (50mph)

# Resources

and 100kph (62mph). All proclaimed routes are numbered (major routes with the prefix B, secondary routes with prefix C, district roads with prefix D and farm roads with prefix P or F), and tourist attractions are generally well marked.

CAR HIRE: Avis, Budget and Imperial are represented in Windhoek with branches at Hosea Kutako International Airport and at Swakopmund or Walvis Bay. Several companies specialize in four-wheel-drive vehicles, and Britz: Namibia rents out campervans. Insurance: Third-party insurance is included in the price of fuel. The excess for damage to hired vehicles is high as most driving is on gravel roads with high accident rates. When making reservations, establish the excess and the renter's responsibility in respect of collision damage waiver insurance.

PETROL: Petrol is available at filling stations throughout Namibia. In Windhoek and some of the larger towns fuel is available 24 hours a day, but in some of the smaller towns and settlements pumps close at 18:00, while restricted hours could apply during weekends. The availability of fuel at some settlements in remote areas is unreliable at times and you should ensure that you have sufficient fuel to get to your destination. In the northwest of Namibia petrol is available only at Ruacana, Sesfontein and Opuwo. Cash only is accepted for petrol in rural areas.

AUTOMOBILE ASSOCIATION OF NAMIBIA: The AAN office is in the Carl List Building, on the corner of Independence Avenue and Fidel Castro Street, tel: (061) 224201. The AA has tow-in service contractors in all major towns. The after-hours breakdown number is: (061) 224201. Maps of Namibia and other southern African countries are also available.

Coach travel: Intercape Mainliner operates a luxury coach service between Windhoek and Walvis Bay, and between Windhoek and Victoria Falls. There are also regular coach departures from the capital to Cape Town and Johannesburg in South Africa.

## What to Wear

During the day dress is usually casual, but in some of the more sophisticated hotel restaurants and bars, jeans, T-shirts and slip-slops are not acceptable in the evening when 'smart casual' clothes are the norm. Early mornings and evenings can be cold during winter (May to September), so pack warm clothing such as trousers, long-sleeved shirts, a jersey or anorak. During the hot summer months (October to April) loose-fitting clothes, a wide-rimmed hat and a raincoat are essential. After rain, temperatures drop by quite a few degrees so include a light jersey for the occasional cool summer evening. Mosquitoes can be troublesome during summer, so remember to pack loose-fitting trousers and long-sleeved shirts to protect legs and arms during the evenings. Warm clothing is necessary throughout the year along the coast where fog and a chilly breeze can create unpleasant conditions.

## Medical Services

It is advisable to take out medical insurance before your departure for Namibia. Windhoek has three private hospitals (the Roman Catholic Hospital in Werner List Street, Medi-Clinic in Erospark and the Rhino Park Private Hospital), there is a Medi-Clinic in Otjiwarongo, and Swakopmund has the Cottage Private Hospital. Walvis Bay has the Welwitschia Hospital. Some churches in the north of the country run hospitals or clinics, and there are state hospitals in major towns. Membership of International SOS, a company which specializes in dealing with medical emergencies countrywide, is highly advisable, tel: (061) 231236, fax: 231254.

DOCTORS: Private doctors in Windhoek are listed under 'Medical practitioners' in the telephone directory.

PHARMACIES: All major towns have pharmacies, usually open during normal business hours; some pharmacies in Windhoek have extended trading hours. In rural areas medication is often available only from the state hospital or clinic.

## Security

As a rule it is quite safe to walk around the streets of Windhoek and other towns after dark without fear of being attacked, although isolated incidents do occur from time to time so some basic precautions are advisable. Avoid looking like the typical tourist, do not carry large amounts of cash on your person and hand valuables in for safekeeping at hotels. In some rural areas petty thieving has become a problem, so do not leave camping gear and other valuables unattended; rather lock them away.

*Information courtesy of*
*the* Globetrotter Guide to Namibia
*by Willie Olivier,*
*published by New Holland Publishers.*